THE ACCIDENTAL ANALYST®

SHOW YOUR DATA WHO'S BOSS™

Eileen McDaniel, PhD

Stephen McDaniel

Please visit us at www.AccidentalAnalyst.com

We will post examples, more ideas and our training seminar schedule over the coming months. Contact us for information about public and on-site seminars and speaking engagements. Don't forget to sign up for our newsletter!

During the two years that Eileen and Stephen worked on this book,
they visited more than 47 cities (some multiple times),
flying one-quarter of a million miles!

They'd like to thank their students from around the world
for all of their ideas and inspiration!

About Tableau maps: www.tableausoftware.com/mapdata

AUTHORS

Eileen McDaniel

Eileen is Co-Founder and Managing Partner of Freakalytics, LLC, specializing in educational materials and analytical training that empower people to get the most out of their data and take decisive action to solve problems in their daily work. She leads the development of training manuals and other publications, consults on short-term marketing research projects, and prepares and presents sessions given at both public conferences and internal company workshops.

As a scientific researcher with a PhD in Ecology, she won multiple awards for excellence in both research and teaching, including one on Capitol Hill from the U.S. Congress. She designed and implemented studies in which she collected and analyzed data from disparate sources to offer novel approaches to resource management. Her research experience evolved into an interest in green or eco-marketing analytics and completion of an MBA Certificate in Marketing Analytics. She is co-author of "***Rapid Graphs with Tableau Software 7***", and the "***Rapid Dashboards Reference Card and App***".

Eileen's unique expertise in science and business led her to realize that although scientists have a formal, step-by-step method to collect and analyze their data, business analysts lack a similar plan. This realization inspired the framework for data analysis used in "***The Accidental Analyst***".

Stephen McDaniel

Stephen is Co-Founder and Principal Analyst of Freakalytics, LLC. He has over 20 years of experience as a statistician, analyst, data architect, instructor, data miner, consultant, software innovator and author. He has been a faculty member at The Data Warehouse Institute (TDWI) and with the American Marketing Association (AMA), developing and teaching hands-on courses and presenting talks on real-world analytic principles and case studies. He has also led and provided vision for data warehousing, business intelligence and advanced analytic teams at Tableau Software, SAS Institute, Brio Technology, Glaxo, Takeda Abbott Pharmaceuticals, Netflix and Loudcloud.

Stephen is lead author of multiple versions of "*SAS for Dummies*™", "*Rapid Graphs with Tableau Software 7*", and the "*Rapid Dashboards Reference Card and App*". At Freakalytics, he was the founder of Tableau's worldwide training program with Eileen, providing public and onsite hands-on analytic training. He has worked with and been an invited instructor at many leading organizations including Target, State Farm, Eli Lilly, IMS Health, Boeing, American Express, Oracle, Australian Government—Intellectual Property Australia, Duke University, Fidelity Investments, US Navy CyberDefense Operations Command, Brown University, The University of Washington at Seattle, The University of California at Berkeley, The Ohio State University and The US Department of the Treasury. Stephen's dream (and Eileen's concern!) is to one day open a wine bar with an extensive chocolate and cheese selection.

TABLE OF CONTENTS

INTRODUCTION

Know where to find the information and how to use it—
That's the secret of success.

—ALBERT EINSTEIN

DATA OVERLOAD

Do you feel like you're drowning in a sea of data? Would you like to take control of your data and analysis, so you can quickly answer your business questions and take action? Do you want to confidently present results and provide solutions to your managers, colleagues, clients and the public?

If so, **The Accidental Analyst: Show Your Data Who's Boss** is for you! Although you didn't plan for a career as a data analyst, you're now in a position where you have to analyze data to be successful. Whether you've been working with data for a few years or are just getting started, you can learn how to analyze your data to find answers to real-world questions. Using illustrated examples, we'll walk you through a clear, step-by-step framework that we call **The Seven C's of Data Analysis**.

Read this book for inspiration, ideas and confidence to begin tackling the problems you face at work. Keep it by your desk as a reference for data organization and analysis techniques. Don't worry, you can continue to use your favorite spreadsheet or data analysis software—this information is not tied to any particular application. Throughout the book, we also explain expert tips, tricks, and shortcuts that took us years of analyzing data to discover and understand.

YOU DON'T NEED TO BE AN EXPERT TO BE SUCCESSFUL: ACCIDENTAL ANALYSTS CAN TAKE CONTROL

Netflix gives you movie recommendations, Amazon suggests products that might interest you, TiVo selects shows for you to watch, the supermarket prints coupons just for you, and an online dating site can match you with a potential mate. All are examples of how companies use data analysis to solve complex problems, make their customers happy, and increase profits along the way. Whether your company has just started analyzing data or maintains a sophisticated data warehouse, you and your colleagues probably know that the future success of the company relies on transforming those data into better decisions.

Because of these well-known uses of data analysis, there are often stories in popular media about how turning data into decisions is the priceless skill of the future. With the explosion of data collection in recent years, even businesspeople that were never trained to deal with data—who we call *accidental analysts*—have to think and work in a new way to be successful. That means that whether you are a sales manager, a marketing director, a human resources specialist, an IT expert, a non-profit manager, an entrepreneur, a government professional or one of many other jobs in business today, you must face the torrent of data head-on and turn it to your advantage.

To put your organization's data to work you don't need to develop sophisticated models like the experts at Netflix or Amazon—that's not the point of this book. You can gain many valuable insights into your business by learning and using basic analysis techniques. Depending on your business, you may want to look at product growth by region, track employee travel expenses, examine growth by product and industry in your sales pipeline, determine usage patterns on your website over time, or assess cost ratios for developing a new product compared to the old one.

To be successful as an analyst, you don't need a computer science degree or an MBA. You also *don't* need complex analytical software or advanced programming skills. If you are familiar with basic analytical tools, such as spreadsheets and graphing software, you can immediately begin using the information and examples in this book to understand how to turn your data into actionable results.

We'd like to emphasize that this book is not about software. Instead, we walk you through the overall analytic process using a clear, concise framework, complete with many illustrations and tricks of the trade we've learned from our extensive experience in analyzing data and in training thousands of analysts. We'll explain how to figure out what questions to ask and what information to share so that you'll not only be more effective in analyzing your data, you'll also be empowered when dealing with managers, colleagues, vendors, students, competitors and the public.

In the rest of this introduction, we describe the keystones, or core characteristics, that are important to being a successful analyst. We outline and summarize the framework of the book, a step-by-step plan called *The Seven C's of Data Analysis* that explains how to organize, analyze, and present your data. We then explain who will find this book most useful. Finally, we review the structure of the book, including important features, so you know what to expect.

WHAT YOU NEED TO SUCCEED:
KEYSTONES FOR ANALYTICAL SUCCESS

Life is not just a series of calculations
and a sum total of statistics,
it's about experience,
it's about participation,
it is something more complex
and more interesting than what is obvious.

—DANIEL LIBESKIND
World-renowned American architect

We've developed a list of keystones that will help you to become a successful analyst. Not every analyst will be great at every keystone, but we believe that everyone can improve at all of them.

You'll need:

- *Passion for helping people solve real-world problems.* This is the most important keystone! We understand that at this point you may be overwhelmed or confused by how to take control of your data, and we hope that our book will help you discover this passion. Once you learn how to prepare and analyze your data to begin to solve your business problems—and also help other people to be more successful in their jobs—you will feel like you are making a difference.

- *Knowledge of your business.* Most of you probably know how your organization or department functions, unless you're new to your job. We also hope that this book will inspire you to look at your role in the context of your business from a different perspective, allowing you to ask questions that you haven't been able to answer before.

- *Exposure to thinking analytically and problem-solving.* Don't worry—you don't need to be a statistician, but you should be able to reason clearly and solve problems logically. Understanding the examples in this book may help you discover that you have more skills, experience, and common sense in this area than you thought.

- *Experience using data to solve problems.* You have more experience using data than you realize since daily life involves processing a constant deluge of data to make decisions. Even if you make a wrong decision, you learn what not to do next time. By following the examples and case studies in this book, you'll begin to understand how to maximize what you get from your data. You'll gain even more experience as you apply those skills and techniques to your everyday work.

- *Familiarity with spreadsheets and graphing software.* Most of you have experience in this area. Since we don't focus on using a software product in this book, you'll be able to take what you learn and apply it to whichever tools your company uses.

- *Effective communication skills.* Analyzing data is only one part of the job—effectively communicating your results is crucial. You need to know your audience, frame the problem clearly, and present the data and analysis in a way that tells a compelling and persuasive story. You'll also want to know and avoid the most common pitfalls in designing tables, graphs, and presentations. We'll cover this topic throughout the book.

- *Support of management and colleagues.* The best decisions can be made only if there is a good analysis to point them out. A good analysis requires a collaborative and interactive relationship between you and your managers and colleagues. It also means that internal company politics come into play, and that's where management support becomes critical. We'll share tips on involving your managers and co-workers in your data analysis, so the results can lead to better decisions and improve the quality of everyone's work.

A FRAMEWORK TO GUIDE YOU: THE SEVEN C'S OF DATA ANALYSIS

Science is a way of thinking much more than it is a body of knowledge.

—CARL SAGAN
Astronomer, best-selling author,
and star of the TV show *Cosmos*

Scientists have developed a step-by-step method to organize their thoughts and guide their analyses. Businesspeople can also benefit from having a framework to follow! We've adapted the method used by scientists to help you analyze real-world problems that you encounter every day in your job. This will help you simplify your analyses and make better decisions for your business. That means more profits for your company, more success and promotions for you—all while cutting down on wasted time and frustration.

We call this framework *The Seven C's of Data Analysis*. This plan will help you figure out what analytical questions are worthwhile for you to ask, demonstrate the techniques you need to find and organize the correct data, guide you through your analysis using examples and case studies, and show you how to effectively communicate the results to your colleagues and clients. It can help make any analysis, from simple to complex, more efficient and worthwhile.

Here is a brief overview of *The Seven C's*, which are demonstrated in detail in the rest of the book.

The Seven C's of Data Analysis

The First C: Choose Your Questions
The single most important step in any analysis is to choose the questions that you're trying to answer, as they provide a clear goal of what you are trying to accomplish. In this C, we describe a general process, along with a case study, of how you can determine the questions of relevance to your project. Choosing questions is often more of a "soft" skill when compared to the later C's, as it involves assessing what's going on in your department or company and incorporating the opinions of your colleagues.

The Second C: Collect Your Data
To take control of your data, first you have to collect the right data for your question and organize it in one place. This C is divided into a **three-step plan**, to help you figure out what data you need, find out where to get them, and combine them into one dataset if they are in different places.

The Third C: Check Out Your Data
This C demonstrates how to become knowledgeable about your dataset by reviewing information about important data items. We've compiled a **data review toolkit** of six tools that are invaluable in accomplishing these tasks. Many business questions can be answered with these tools.

The Fourth C: Clean Up Your Data
No company's data are perfect, but you can do a few things to clean up the mistakes and inaccuracies in your data as much as possible. In this C, we include **Do-It-Yourself Quick Fixes** for issues that you can clean up yourself, and some ways to identify and possibly even fix more extensive, company-wide problems.

The Fifth C: Chart Your Analysis

Most business questions that you will encounter can be answered by displaying your data in the appropriate chart, which can be a table in a spreadsheet or a graph. We organize this C into a list of **common business scenarios** and which charts are useful in solving them.

The Sixth C: Customize Your Analysis

For questions that you are unable to answer up to this point, you may need to focus on very specific data by customizing your charts. We demonstrate this C by using a **realistic case-study approach**, in which an analyst is in a series of business meetings with colleagues, answering their questions on the spot.

The Seventh C: Communicate Your Results

After completing your analysis, you have one more step: communicating your results in an email, memo, slide show, report, or group meeting. This is the C where the information that you learned in all the other C's comes together. To assess if your presentation is getting the job done, we've included a list of **benchmarks**.

IS THIS BOOK FOR YOU? WHAT CAN YOU GET OUT OF IT?

Accidental analysts are everywhere in business. They can be in sales, marketing, human resources, customer relations, IT, real estate, facilities, education, non-profit work, or anywhere else where data affect (or should affect) decision-making. If you are feeling overwhelmed and frustrated by the waves of data coming at you every day, or could just use some help getting started, this book is for you. However, more experienced analysts may also learn valuable information.

You can immediately use the clear, step-by-step framework to take control of and analyze your data. You can benefit from our strategies for overcoming more intangible challenges such as interacting with co-workers to understand their viewpoints and communicating your work and ideas effectively. These techniques will allow you to succeed as a data analyst, accidental or not!

The material in this book is based on the decades of experience and education that the three of us collectively have in analyzing data. We also have taught many students how to think about analysis, analyze their data, and present their results—and have learned a lot from them. We listened to their interests and concerns, and discovered that students from all types of business have similar experiences and frustrations. We have incorporated these issues throughout the book.

This book can be used for both inspiration and as a reference. You may want to read through it the first time to get ideas and pick up some useful tips, tricks, and shortcuts. There is a lot of information in this book, so you won't be able to remember it all from the first reading, but hopefully you'll begin to improve upon your own work right away. Then, you can keep it by your desk as a reference for data organization and analytical techniques, so the framework and details are always at your fingertips.

Important Points About This Book (so you won't be surprised):

- *The goal of this book is to help people who haven't received extensive training in analysis to become more effective in their daily work.* If you are an advanced or expert analyst, this book is not written for you, although you may find many useful tips and tricks. However, you probably work with accidental analysts, so you may find the approach of the book enlightening, helpful in training and advising aspiring analysts, and worth recommending to them.

- *We focus on the step-by-step process of organizing, analyzing, and sharing your data, so you can quickly answer your or others' business questions.* We use data that people in any business can understand, such as sales, profit, and number of customers, as it would be impossible to cover every business question for every reader.

- *Since the point of this book is to take action and solve your problems using the quickest and easiest analytical methods, we don't discuss theoretical concepts or even statistical methods such as forecasting or modeling.* There are many good books out there that cover these advanced topics, and we've included a short list of them in *Further Reading* at the end of the book.

- *This book describes the analytical process, so it does not focus on any particular analysis or graphing software package (although we assume that most of you are familiar with Microsoft Excel).* Therefore, you can use what you learn in this book in just about any software your company uses.

Analysis Software Applications

Popular analysis tools beyond Microsoft Excel and Microsoft Access include: Business Objects, Cognos, JMP, Microstrategy, QlikView, R, SAS, SPSS, Tableau and Tibco Spotfire.

THE LAYOUT OF THE BOOK

The general structure of the book is simple—we've divided it into The Seven C's of Data Analysis, listed earlier in this introduction. There also is an introductory section, **Data, Data, Data**, before the three C's specific to data gathering and clean-up (**The Second, Third and Fourth C's**) and an introductory section, **Analysis in Action**, before the two C's that focus on data analysis (**The Fifth and Sixth C's**). Each individual C has an introduction, an outline, the topic covered in depth, and a recap at the end. Throughout, we've included real-world business questions and abbreviated case studies to reinforce our points. We've also added a plethora of illustrations to demonstrate the content.

In addition, there are **three types of sidebar boxes** with supplemental information to emphasize tips or hazards or to make you aware of advanced topics.

Three Types of Sidebars

Helpful Hint
Shortcuts or useful tips.

Heads Up
Situations in which people often take a wrong turn.

FYI
Information that may be useful to know but is beyond the scope of this book.

Here's our first sidebar to demonstrate:

FYI

You may have heard of the term **business intelligence**, or **BI**.

A simple definition of business intelligence is the use of specialized software to gather and analyze data with the purpose of making informed business decisions.

We've also added vertical tabs on the right-hand side of each page of the Seven C's. The tabs have abbreviated names representing each C, which are highlighted on the matching pages, for easy reference.

They look like this:

choose questions

collect data
check
clean

chart analysis
custom

communicate results

RECAP OF THE INTRODUCTION

- More than likely, you didn't start your career expecting to be a data analyst. But now, through choice or circumstance, it's what you've become—an **accidental analyst**.

- You are facing a **sea of data** and would like to take control by turning your data into decisions that will make you and your company successful. You may feel confused, frustrated, or simply need help getting oriented and organized.

- This book provides a **strategy of attack,** by offering ideas to get you started as well as a reference to keep at your desk for specific problems in dealing with your data and analysis.

- Our list of **keystones** for analytical success:

  — Passion for helping people solve real-world problems

  — Knowledge of your business

  — Exposure to thinking analytically and problem-solving

  — Experience using data to solve problems

  — Familiarity with spreadsheets and graphing software

  — Effective communication skills

  — Support of management and colleagues

- The framework of the book—The Seven C's of Data Analysis:

    - The First C: Choose Your Questions

    - Data, Data, Data: Introduction to The Second, Third and Fourth C's

    - The Second C: Collect Your Data

    - The Third C: Check Out Your Data

    - The Fourth C: Clean Up Your Data

    - Analysis in Action: Introduction to The Fifth and Sixth C's

    - The Fifth C: Chart Your Analysis

    - The Sixth C: Customize Your Analysis

    - The Seventh C: Communicate Your Results

- Our intended readers are not advanced or expert analysts, so we don't cover theoretical concepts or advanced techniques such as modeling or forecasting (although these can be beneficial for more complex problems), but even advanced analysts may pick up useful tips and tricks or information on how to help colleagues who are accidental analysts.

- This book focuses on the process of analyzing data, not on any particular software, so you can use the information no matter which analytical tools you select or already have installed.

Great—now that you know what this book is about, you're ready to start showing your data who's boss! Onward to *The First C: Choose Your Questions*.

THE FIRST C: CHOOSE YOUR QUESTIONS

The quality of an answer depends
on the quality of the question.

—COMMON SAYING AMONG DATA ANALYSTS

The single most important step in any relevant analysis is to choose the questions that you are trying to answer. While this may sound obvious, it is an ongoing challenge for most analysts (including us) to stay on track by finding answers to the right questions needed to solve the problem at hand. Creating a list of questions clarifies your ultimate goals for your project, and is the best way to make sure that you are not "drifting off course" during the remaining 6 C's of your analysis.

In today's complex world, people in all departments and levels of a company are using data to make decisions. A great analyst needs to be much more than technically adept, because it's necessary to collaborate with others in order to determine what questions need to be answered. To start any project, you must assess what's going on within your company or department, so choosing questions is more of a "soft" skill when compared to the later steps of analysis, requiring a combination of art and science. Since it is a soft skill, it is often the most difficult one to master, so we will walk you through the typical thought processes behind starting your analysis, including ways to encourage input and gain support from your managers and colleagues.

choose questions

collect data | check | clean

chart | custom analysis

communicate results

Helpful Hint

If you are interested in learning the technical details of the process of analyzing data, don't worry.

You will learn plenty of them in the rest of the book, complete with illustrations.

Also, you may want to re-read this C after you read the rest of the book—you'll probably have new insights on how to choose the best questions.

In this chapter, we describe a general process of how you can determine the question(s) of relevance to your project. We mainly focus on the less complex situation in which you're answering the question for yourself, and then use this information to make a data-based decision for the business that you will present to others. In this case, it is possible that your managers, co-workers, or customers will give you a general idea of the problem area that needs to be analyzed.

We've divided this process into three steps:
1. Relax!
2. Gather Information
3. Select Your Questions

Then, we demonstrate the steps using a simple case study. Later in this C, we address the added complexity of starting an analysis project when someone else is the final decision-maker, ending with a short case study.

TAKE CHARGE WHEN YOU ARE MAKING THE DECISION

Step 1. Relax!

If I had eight hours to chop down a tree,
I'd spend six sharpening my axe.

—ABRAHAM LINCOLN
President of the U.S. during the American Civil War

Take it Easy:
Don't skip ahead – time spent on this overlooked "C"
is the secret to success

There is a tendency for people to rush through this step so they can spend more time on the "real work" of collecting and analyzing data! However, choosing the right question(s) is not only the first C, it is also the most important C, because it guides the entire analysis (and is the reason you are doing it in the first place). So you want to make sure that you spend enough time assessing the problem to adequately identify what you need to find out. The upfront investment in forming useful, clear questions will save you a lot of time and frustration by avoiding unnecessary analysis, and even save you the embarrassment of not having a solution to the real problem at the end of your analysis.

Get Started:
Locate the general problem that requires analysis

Bosses, co-workers, or even customers of your business may need help solving an issue or problem. Although they can describe it in general, they may lack the time or ability to explain the details.

For instance, your colleague may notice that gift basket sales to women are down and asks you to find out why. She actually may be seeking a way to improve marketing to women, but doesn't state the problem this way. Or she may be able to tell you the specific goal, such as decreasing waste in product packaging or the number of calls to customer service. Often, she relies on you to do the legwork of specifying the exact question(s) of relevance before doing the analysis and coming up with a reasonable course of action.

At other times, you may be the decision-maker managing an area of business (based on your job description, or maybe it just needs to be done and you are stuck with it by default), and you notice that there is a problem that needs to be corrected. If you are not sure how to fix it, you must look further into the problem in order to form good questions.

Target Audience:
Who will be acting on the decision that you make?

One way to consider the importance and nature of the problem at hand is to determine if the analysis will be used for **strategic**, **operational**, or **analytical** purposes in your business. At first, these may seem like technical terms, but you've probably had experience with these situations in your work.

Strategic

If the results of the analysis will be used by executives, middle management, or business owners, the decisions made will probably affect long-term priorities for the business (often spanning months or even years). For example, they want to know if year-to-date sales in each of the company's three product lines have met the target amount, which is a 10% increase compared to the same time period last year. They are trying to decide if they should allocate more of the budget to marketing or hire more salespeople to increase sales in a particular product line versus another.

This is a strategic decision, which is usually based on less complex analysis and simple, clear presentation of results relative to stated company goals. Since executives typically review the results of strategic analyses on a monthly or quarterly basis, they do not want a lot of details for their review. Instead, they prefer some information about similar situations over time periods in the past (for instance, the first quarter of this year versus the first quarter of last year).

Heads Up
The best companies support a culture where strategic decisions are the result of great ideas combined with business knowledge and data. Many companies are still in the process of developing an environment where data are incorporated into strategic decisions.

Operational

Operational decisions usually involve monitoring live systems, such as overall data center performance or how well a call center is handling customer issues, to identify key problem areas. As a result, teams typically require a summary of performance in the past few days or hours relative to their expected performance to ensure that all is going well. When there are problems, operational people may need to know the "layered" details, or the details behind the details, to help them find and correct issues. Operational analysis results in more concrete results than strategic analysis.

Analytical

If the decision is oriented at an analytical audience, it will likely be used by analysts investigating key issues and possible courses of action. An example is an analyst investigating the reasons behind a drop in sales in the last quarter, as compared to the same quarter last year, to find possible solutions. These analyses typically include high-level summaries and detailed reviews "below the covers" to explore possible causes of problems. Analysts often spend significant time exploring these layers by several analyses that progressively reveal more information with each layer of data. This type of analysis may provide definite results for a problem or simply point you in a general direction.

Helpful Hint

You should also think about the personality, skills, and time constraints of the colleagues that you are helping.

For example, if your question and analysis involve complex technical details, and your colleague is always on the move and just looking for a general idea of what to do, you may be providing more information than he or she wants or needs. Also, you may waste a lot of your time creating a sophisticated analysis when a simple answer would be enough.

Step 2. Gather Information

A good decision is based on knowledge and not on numbers.

—PLATO
Classical Greek philosopher,
key to the establishment of
Western philosophy and science

Learn From the Past:
Collect information that is already known about the problem

It is amazing what you can learn by simply talking to, and more importantly, listening to other people with knowledge of the general issue. During this time you can learn what they know (this is a crucial point that we'll emphasize throughout the book) while gaining an ally for when you need help during the analysis. You also can incorporate their opinions into what you already know about the problem. Listening to others is especially helpful if you are new to the job or the company.

By speaking with others, you may be able to find out what relevant analyses have been done in the past, the results, if and how these results led to decisions that were actually implemented, and if the project ended up as a success. In general, other people often will help you develop great ideas of what to do. Perhaps one of the most important things these conversations will tell you, which often isn't documented, are the analyses that "failed". Analysis projects can fail for many reasons, including poorly designed questions, incomplete analyses, poor communications, or decisions that were never carried out due to company politics or other limitations.

These people may also be able to direct you to previous reports or presentations, so you don't waste time looking through irrelevant paperwork or re-doing old analyses. They also may be able to tell you where the relevant data sources are located, which will save time later in your analysis. Even if they tell you that nothing has been done on this issue in the past, this is useful information, because it tells you that any well-designed analysis and decision that you come up with is likely superior to what has been done before.

Heads Up

Incorporate all the information that you've discovered during the gathering process and use your own judgment before you determine what question will guide your analysis.

For instance, just because the company has always done things a certain way doesn't mean that it's the best way.

Play Well with Others:
Bring colleagues on board

In addition to finding out the history of the problem, gathering input from others has another powerful benefit for you. It is usually a good idea to ask for people's opinions, particularly if they will be involved in gathering the data, performing the analysis, or implementing the decision resulting from the analysis. Never underestimate the importance of getting people on board with your work! They are more likely to do so if they feel their views are understood from the start and taken into account since they will then have a stake in the success of your analysis.

Heads Up

Be aware that there is a fine line between gathering people's input and pestering them.

The goal of this book is for your boss and colleagues to be happy to see you, not to run when they see you coming down the hall!

Expand the Possibilities:
Avoid selecting questions based only on the usual data

The temptation at this stage in the process is to think about the problem at hand through the limited lens of the data you or your team "typically" uses for this area. This restriction can limit your success in making better decisions and constrains you from considering new and innovative analyses that may be possible.

In most cases, determine the questions to ask under the assumption that you could obtain all the data you need. You may be surprised to find that with a little searching you actually can incorporate new, invaluable data. However, if it turns out that optimal data collection isn't possible due to time or budget constraints, computer limitations, etc., then you can adjust which data are used. Even considering and addressing these limitations can be part of your final presentation to colleagues—and may inspire improvements in data collection in your business.

That being said, although you shouldn't base the decision to be made on the data you already have easily available, we realize that in the real world you often are in a rush to do analyses. If you are short on time, spend at least a few minutes considering possible enhancements or key data that would make your analysis more valuable. Discussing this possibility with your team may even create an atmosphere of innovation around your data collection efforts.

Step 3. Select your questions

The best way to have a good idea is to have a lot of ideas.

—LINUS PAULING
Two-time Nobel Laureate,
one of the greatest scientists of the 20th century

Put It All Out There:
Create a list of the questions that might address the problem at hand

At this point everything is fair game—add every question that you think might possibly improve or solve the problem at hand. It usually helps to organize your thoughts by dividing the general issue into topics, and then listing possible decisions to be made under each topic.

By creating a simple list on paper, in a Word document, or in a spreadsheet, it will be easier to spot any major gaps and identify which questions may overlap with each other. Try to make the questions specific rather than vague. You may even want to share this simple list with colleagues to give them an opportunity to contribute or clarify questions. If it's on a whiteboard, you may even interest people walking by who will join in.

Reduce, Reuse, Recycle:
Optimize your list of questions

Now it's time to refine the list so you have only the best ones remaining. Unless you are very new to your team, you can probably do this in 20 or 30 minutes.

1. Reduce by eliminating unrelated, inefficient or impractical questions

First, you need to remove the least useful questions. Does the question pass this point-by-point inspection for quality control?

Is the question…

Related to the problem at hand?

It may be a good question, but if doesn't help you solve the current issue, get rid of it.

Relevant to the department or person that is most affected by or interested in the final decision?

If you are solving a marketing problem, you may want to defer questions that require the involvement of another department, such as finance, in order to be successful. In an ideal world the best decision would be implemented, regardless of the department(s) involved—but this is the real world.

Focused on an option that is substantial enough to have a real impact on the problem?

Keep your overall goal in mind. For instance, your question may be how to cut down on packaging waste for your company. You know from a previous analysis that Product Line X contributes just 1% to waste. So, don't focus on that product line if there are only three product lines at your company.

Realistic because the solution would fit in with the current situation and not require a radical and quick change?

Remember that for most projects the company can only change so much based on one analysis. Therefore, drastic changes are unrealistic, at least in a short time frame, unless management specifically asked you to examine possible unorthodox approaches.

For example, if your question is "What would be the impact on sales if we double the number of advertising billboards in the next quarter?", but your company just cut the marketing budget in half, the question most likely is not worth your time.

A good fit for the corporate culture?

If your company is a web-based retailer, then examining the possibility of opening retail locations is likely a waste of your time, and may even irritate your decision-makers.

2. Reuse useful questions from the past

If you or someone else has done a similar analysis in the past, add those questions to the mix. Remember to evaluate the questions using the point-by-point inspection in the *Reduce* section.

Helpful Hint

Often the same issues arise repeatedly, so it may help you to start building a pool of standard questions in a spreadsheet or Word document (even if you don't use them in this analysis).

---

3. Recycle by revising improperly worded questions

The general point of a question may be valid, but it may be inaccurately stated.

Here's a simple example. The original question is: "How much has profit decreased our advertising budget?"

However, the question should be: "How much has our advertising budget decreased profit?"

Again, put the new question through the point-by-point inspection in the *Reduce* section.

Best Foot Forward, Please: Choose the best questions to analyze

There isn't enough time to answer all your questions, so you need to organize your list to figure out which ones to focus on. This is often the hardest step of the First C. We typically rank questions in order of importance, from most valuable to least valuable, while taking into account the following constraints:

1. How direct or easy is it to implement the likely solution if you answer the question?

2. Who will take action with the results of your analysis?
   Will they understand your line of attack?

3. Do you have enough time to find, organize, and analyze the data to answer the question?

4. Will there be enough time to implement the recommendation from the possible solutions?

5. Will this question require the assistance of other people?
   Is it expertise that you don't have?
   Is the question valuable enough that you will be able to acquire the needed time from the experts in your company?

6. Is there a budget for your analysis?
   If so, what are the budget limitations?
   For example, if your question requires purchasing third-party data or software you don't have, is this possible?

Some of the questions can be answered later, or you can do a more in-depth analysis of the most important questions in lieu of answering a long list of less-relevant questions. While it is tough to do, creating an outline with the most useful questions at the top of the list helps you to begin to see a path to completion.

Walk through the steps: The First C Case Study

This simple case study demonstrates the steps of choosing your questions.

Get Started

Jeff is a new analyst at an online pet supply company. The sales manager of pet food products approaches him with a problem. In the last month, pet food sales were up 30%, but dog treat sales were down 10%. Can he figure out possible causes?

Target Audience

The target audience for Jeff's analysis is the sales manager for pet food.

Learn From the Past

Jeff speaks with his colleagues to find out the last time dog treat sales were down. He discovers that this occurred in January. When he asks them why, they tell him that people give dog treats as holiday presents in December. He asks if there was any other time sales were down, and no one remembers this happening.

Play Well with Others

Jeff updates his boss about what's going on. Also, before he starts the analysis, he brings the issue up at his group's weekly review meeting to get input. He is checking to see if someone else has either investigated the problem or plans to, so he doesn't duplicate effort.

Expand the Possibilities

Jeff wants to know more about the problem before he works on the data. He looks at the pet food web pages. He wants to know what the shopping experience is like for the customer. Maybe dog treats were on the home page last month and now they're not, while regular dog food is? He was hoping to solve the problem at this point, but after researching relevant issues, he is still not sure of the cause.

Put It All Out There

Jeff compiles a list of all the questions he can think of that are relevant to the issue:

1. Was there a shortage in dog treats in the inventory for the last few months?
2. Were there any special offers for pet food or dog treats in the last few months that might have affected sales?
3. Treats aren't a necessity, so have other unnecessary dog accessories shown any changes in buying behavior?
4. Are there new pet food products that might have increased pet food sales?
5. Did our competitors have the same issue?
6. Did the dog treat manufacturer have a coupon that is now expired?
7. Examining sales of dog treats over the past few years by month, is there a seasonal pattern by month or time of year (beyond the commonly known "January effect")?

Reduce, Reuse, Recycle

Jeff then eliminates or rewords some of the questions, and adds a relevant question (#8) that a colleague investigated in the past:

1. Was there a shortage in dog treats in the inventory for the last few months?
2. Were there any special offers for pet food or dog treats in the last few months that might have affected sales?
3. Treats aren't a necessity, so have other unnecessary dog accessories shown any changes in buying behavior?
4. Are there new pet food products that might have increased pet food sales?
5. ~~Did our competitors have the same issue?~~ *Can't find out this detailed information, but can reword as: Did our competitors have a big sale?*
6. ~~Did the dog treat manufacturer have a coupon that is now expired?~~ *Hard to find this out.*
7. Examining sales of dog treats over the past few years by month, is there a seasonal pattern by month or time of year (beyond the commonly known "January effect")?
8. Was there a manufacturer's recall of poor-quality dog treats in the last few months?

Best Foot Forward, Please

Jeff prioritizes the questions with the ones that he thinks are most useful first:

1. Were there any special offers for pet food or dog treats in the last few months that might have affected sales?
2. Did our competitors have a big sale?
3. Was there a shortage in dog treats in the inventory for the last few months?
4. Was there a manufacturer's recall of poor-quality dog treats in the last few months?
5. Treats aren't a necessity, so have other unnecessary dog accessories shown any changes in buying behavior?
6. Examining sales of dog treats over the past few years by month, is there a seasonal pattern by month or time of year (beyond the commonly known "January effect")?
7. Are there new pet food products that might have increased pet food sales?

Now Jeff has a list of questions that he can start to analyze, beginning at the top!

PLAN OF ATTACK WHEN SOMEONE ELSE IS THE DECISION-MAKER

What's their point? Translate a request into a question

If you are very lucky, decision-makers can explain to you the decisions that they need to make. Presumably, your analysis can help them have more confidence in their "gut" feelings or possibly steer them in another direction. Ideally, they will clearly articulate the problem and explain it sufficiently so that it makes sense to you. If this happens, then you can celebrate and move on to *The Second C: Collect Your Data.*

However, another scenario is typical: you are presented with general issues and need to translate what the decision-maker wants into questions that she can take action on once you have answers at the end of your analysis. Often, she can't quite explain the issue to you.

Even if she thinks she knows, you may be unsure if she is asking the right questions, or even know that she isn't. There are variations on this scenario—for instance, we've had clients whose colleagues show them a graph and request an analysis that results in a similar graph, although it may not be applicable to the actual problem at hand. Or colleagues may stay in their "comfort zone" by asking the same questions about a particular problem area, but the questions need to be updated based upon new developments.

Although this may be difficult, the first step to "translating" what your colleague is asking for is to look at the issue from his or her point of view.

To translate, there are three crucial questions that you should ask yourself:

1. *What does she care about?* For example, is she in Sales, Finance, or Human Resources? Is she in charge of customer acquisition or customer retention? Does she have a year-end closing soon, or is she just checking to see how receivables are doing?
2. *How do you make her more successful?* What will make her more effective in her job, helping her to deliver results to her managers or colleagues?
3. *What are the goals of the team and company?* Is the company trying to open new stores or close old ones? Become environmentally sustainable?

Even if you don't understand exactly what she is asking for when you speak to her, write down everything you can during the meeting, and as soon as possible afterwards. Listen for cues, especially "points of reference" that she typically refers to in her explanations.

Here are some examples of what we mean by points of reference, including what the decision-maker might say and the possible translation that you can act upon.

Point of Reference (cues underlined)	Translation
Sales not on **target**	versus **target**
New products not doing well	versus **target** or **previous products**
Hard to find the **best** sales leads	Needs sales leads **ranked in order of importance**
Expenses are **out of line**	versus **target** or versus **historic norms**
Too many **underutilized** servers in our data center	**capacity** versus **expected performance**

Helpful Hint

Even if you collaborated with the decision-maker to choose the questions, sometimes she will tell you later that they aren't the right ones.

This may be frustrating for both of you, especially if you're far along in the analytic process. Remain calm and try to assess how far off the mark you are by asking her what information she needed to know, but couldn't get from your analysis.

Role-play: Find out what the decision-maker cares about

Since translating what people want into questions that you can analyze is such a difficult skill, here we'll walk you through a few examples. Jeff, our analyst, is meeting with different members of the sales department.

- Vice President (VP) of Sales

The VP asks Jeff:

"Are we finally meeting our monthly sales numbers?"

Jeff translates this as:

"Are sales doing better this month when compared to our monthly sales target? Show me this month and the last few months for context."

- Regional Sales Director of the West

The Sales Director of the West asks Jeff:

"Is the marketing campaign in California worth the money?"

Jeff thinks this means:

"Are sales in California picking up since the marketing campaign was launched? How much, relative to the cost of the campaign?"

- Salesperson for Southern California

The salesperson for Southern California asks:

"Am I effectively following up on my recent sales leads?"

Jeff translates this as a reference to how timely the salesperson has been in following up:

"How many of my open sales opportunities from last month have I spoken with this month? How many from the past quarter?"

As you can see, people at different levels of the same team will often request more details as you move further down the team, starting with upper management. Often, all their questions can be answered using the same data sources, but they need the data analyzed in different ways.

By asking questions of direct relevance to the audience at hand, your work becomes much clearer and more relevant to the people you seek to help. Additionally, it becomes much easier to identify a set of "core" analyses for your job that you quickly can repeat over time.

Heads Up

It is important to remember that at any point in your analysis, you are able to go back to earlier steps if necessary, because analysis is a cyclical process.

For instance, you may discover that none of your questions have good answers that help you solve your problem, so you need to go back to the drawing board and come up with a new list. When you do this, be careful not to skip steps such as running the new list of questions through the point-by-point inspection for quality control.

Visit **http://www.AccidentalAnalyst.com** *to sign up for our newsletter for information about upcoming live training, webinars, tips, books and more!*

RECAP OF THE FIRST C: CHOOSE YOUR QUESTIONS

- Choosing your questions is the crucial first step in any analysis, and returning to those questions throughout the course of your work is the best way to keep things on track.

- Either you are doing the analysis for yourself, so you are the decision-maker that will determine how to correct the problem, or you are doing the analysis for someone else who is the decision-maker (the first situation is usually much easier).

- The three steps in choosing your questions are:

    — Relax:
    figure out the problem and who will act on the solution

    — Gather information:
    find whatever's known about the problem

    — Select your questions:
    create and prioritize a list of questions

- Review the simple case study, where Jeff the analyst comes up with questions.

- Translating colleagues' requests into questions that you can act upon is quite difficult, so look for points of reference and what their goals are.

- Review the role-playing case study, where Jeff the analyst determines what different colleagues need from him.

DATA, DATA, DATA:
THE SECOND, THIRD AND FOURTH C'S

Data, Data, Data!
I can't make bricks without clay!

—SHERLOCK HOLMES

Great—you've made it this far! Even expert analysts typically agree that *The First C: Choose Your Questions* is often the most difficult step. If you've managed to specify your final goal, along with the questions and answers that you need to achieve it—or even harder, what someone else's goal and questions are—then you've made a lot of progress. In the next section of this book, you'll find a game plan of how to take control of your data.

We often hear from businesspeople that they have so much data, they don't know what to do with them all, leaving them feeling overwhelmed and confused. They frequently have a hard time figuring out which data they need for the analysis at hand. Other data headaches include being afraid of using the wrong data, not using all of the right data, or not even being able to find the right data. And once they find what data they want, they often lack even basic descriptions of what they have relative to their analysis, so they are unable to answer their own or others' simple questions. They also are not sure whether the data are "good" data, or data that contain hidden flaws and mistakes that need to be addressed.

People are smart to be concerned about these things, since it is challenging to perform a successful analysis if you don't have high-quality data. The next three C's will show you how to obtain high-quality data.

THE SECOND C: COLLECT YOUR DATA

Find and use the best data that are relevant for the decision at hand, from data sources that are currently available to you or that you can reasonably obtain. This C includes avoiding the wrong data.

THE THIRD C: CHECK OUT YOUR DATA

Review and understand the data you've selected to paint a general picture before you begin your in-depth analysis.

THE FOURTH C: CLEAN UP YOUR DATA

Find and fix mistakes and problems, or at least be aware of the limitations of the data you will use in your analysis.

Heads Up

These three data steps often require more time than you might think.

With experience, you will gain a better sense of how much time the Data C's require, but there have been countless times we've said, or worked with other analysts who said, "Getting the data ready took more time than anything else."

Data preparation is a frustrating reality of data analysis, but doing a good job is worth it. Just like investing the time to choose your questions, this **will** save you a lot of time later in the process. It can also help you avoid embarrassment or a lack of confidence in your analysis because someone points out that your results look strange. These unexpected results can happen when you discover that you used the wrong data or overlooked correcting a key data problem. Additionally, once you have inventoried, organized, and cleaned up your data, you will have a much easier time using them in future analyses.

FYI

In the business world, people often have little or no control over what types of data are collected and often base their analyses on what's available.

This is a different situation than what most scientists typically face, where they design the experiment and choose the necessary data before they collect them— although more and more in today's world of automated data collection, they also must base their experiments on existing data.

THE SECOND C: COLLECT YOUR DATA

It is a capital mistake to theorize before one has data.

—SIR ARTHUR CONAN DOYLE
Author of Sherlock Holmes stories

To take control of your data, first you have to collect the right data for your question and organize them in one place. To help you accomplish this, *The Second C: Collect Your Data* is divided into three steps:

STEP 1: IDENTIFY YOUR DATA

Assess what data you need for your analysis.

STEP 2: INVENTORY YOUR DATA

Figure out where to get the data you need, while also keeping an inventory of your datasets that you can use for current and future analyses.

STEP 3: INTEGRATE YOUR DATA

In case the necessary data are in more than one data file, you will need to combine or integrate multiple datasets.

STEP 1. IDENTIFY YOUR DATA: MATCH THE DATA WITH YOUR QUESTIONS

You can have data without information,
but you cannot have information without data.

—DANIEL KEYS MORAN
Science fiction author and
computer programmer

What do we mean by data? **Data** are any type of information regarding your business or organization that can be collected and compiled in a spreadsheet. **Data items** are "pieces" of data that describe particular attributes of your dataset, such as *customer name*, *sale amount in dollars*, and *date of purchase*. Data items are also commonly called **fields**, **measures**, **metrics**, **columns**, or **variables**. Data can be captured and accessed from a wide variety of systems, including direct entry in a spreadsheet, web servers, cash registers, utility meters, sales systems, inventory systems, third-party providers such as credit bureaus, and many other sources.

FYI

Although the word "data" is often used as a singular word in conversation and news media, it is technically a plural word, as in "the data are missing".

In order to select the right data items for your question and analysis, you need to identify what kinds of data items you have and which questions they can help you answer.

For the purposes of this book, we divide data items into two major types: **categorical** and **numerical**. **Categorical** data items organize data into groups, and answer the questions *Who?*, *What?*, *Where?*, and *When?*. **Numerical** data items are numbers that can be used in calculations, such as addition or multiplication, and answer the questions *How much?*, *How many?*, and *How long?*. More details about categorical versus numerical data items can be found in the boxes on the following pages.

Categorical Data Items

- Also known as categories, headers, groupings or dimensions

- Organize data into groups

- Answer the questions:

  - *Who?* customer name, customer ID, salesperson, gender
  - *What?* product type, loyalty club member level, opinion
  - *Where?* store location, customer address, zip code, region, sales channel
  - *When?* date, month, year

- Categorical data that contain numbers are used as labels, and typically are not used in calculations (such as addition or multiplication):

  - Examples include customer ID or zip code
  - Your software might identify these as numbers, so you will have to change these to labels or text fields in your dataset
  - One exception: dates, months (if represented by numbers, such as December = 12) and years may be subtracted to find the amount of time that has passed, but they usually aren't added, multiplied, etc.

- Categorical data are often assigned numeric codes for data entry or simplicity of data storage; for instance:

  - Female = 1 and Male = 2
  - Platinum customer = 1, Gold customer = 2, and Silver customer = 3
  - Treat these as categorical items in your analysis

Numerical Data Items

- Also known as numeric measures, measures, or metrics

- Typically used in everyday calculations, such as sum or average

- Answer the questions:

  - *How much?* product price, sales, profit, expenses
  - *How many?* number of customers, number of stores, purchase quantity
  - *How long?* number of minutes, days, months, years

- Not all numerical items can be used in every type of calculation; for example:

  - It would be incorrect to add up last year's inventory count with this year's inventory count because the sum of inventory in two separate years is meaningless (you may be counting the same items twice)
  - However, the average of the inventory across the two years might be meaningful when planning for the next year

- Values of numerical data items can be:

  - **discrete**, or limited to certain values; number of customers can be 1,2,3, etc., not 1.5
  - **continuous**, or uninterrupted; dollar amount can be $5 or $100, but also can be $6.32 or $95.68

Take a look at this clip of a spreadsheet.

Data types: categorical versus numerical data items

	A	B	C	D	E	F	G
1	Order Date	State	Customer ID	Customer Segment	Product Short Name	Quantity	Total Item Amount
3	12-Apr-10	ME	201775	Luxury Estate	'Baby Got Back' Cotton Dog Tank Top	1	$15
4	14-Apr-10	NJ	102635	Ad Referral	SnooZZy Chocolate Cozy Crate Bed	2	$58
5	23-Apr-10	VA	683822	Luxury Estate	'Baby Got Back' Cotton Dog Tank Top	1	$15
6	24-Apr-10	WA	83039	Big Spender	Bad To Da Bone Dog Tank Top	1	$15
7	23-May-10	IL	877928	Luxury Estate	Sparkle Paw 18-inch Dog Collar	1	$13
8	16-Aug-10	TX	218681	Luxury Estate	SnooZZy Caramel Pillow Talk 1000 Pet Bed	1	$24
9	10-Sep-10	MD	595300	Ad Referral	XX-Large Fleece-lined Dog Boots	1	$25
10	10-Sep-10	TN	619793	Ad Referral	SnooZZy Chocolate 6000 Cozy Comforter	1	$48
11	12-Sep-10	IL	766530	Big Spender	Pet Gear Indoor Pet Ramp	1	$55
12	31-Oct-10	VA	466047	Luxury Estate	Ruff Ruff and Meow Lucky Charm Dog's Tank Top	1	$15
13	31-Dec-10	CA	514145	Ad Referral	Precision Pet SnooZZy Crate Bed 3000	1	$28
14	25-Jan-11	MI	783323	Luxury Estate	Rabbit Resort Medium Kennel	1	$49
15	17-Feb-11	IN	978034	Ultimate Web Hunter	SnooZZy 1000 Original Fleece Bumper Bed	1	$19

In this sample spreadsheet, the categorical data items are *Customer ID* and *Customer Segment* (Who?), *Product Short Name* (What?), *State* (Where?), and *Order Date* (When?).

Data types: categorical data items

	A	B	C	D	E	F	G
1	Order Date	State	Customer ID	Customer Segment	Product Short Name	Quantity	Total Item Amount
3	12-Apr-10	ME	201775	Luxury Estate	'Baby Got Back' Cotton Dog Tank Top	1	$15
4	14-Apr-10	NJ	102635	Ad Referral	SnooZZy Chocolate Cozy Crate Bed	2	$58
5	23-Apr-10	VA	683822	Luxury Estate	'Baby Got Back' Cotton Dog Tank Top	1	$15
6	24-Apr-10	WA	83039	Big Spender	Bad To Da Bone Dog Tank Top	1	$15
7	23-May-10	IL	877928	Luxury Estate	Sparkle Paw 18-inch Dog Collar	1	$13
8	16-Aug-10	TX	218681	Luxury Estate	SnooZZy Caramel Pillow Talk 1000 Pet Bed	1	$24
9	10-Sep-10	MD	595300	Ad Referral	XX-Large Fleece-lined Dog Boots	1	$25
10	10-Sep-10	TN	619793	Ad Referral	SnooZZy Chocolate 6000 Cozy Comforter	1	$48
11	12-Sep-10	IL	766530	Big Spender	Pet Gear Indoor Pet Ramp	1	$55
12	31-Oct-10	VA	466047	Luxury Estate	Ruff Ruff and Meow Lucky Charm Dog's Tank Top	1	$15
13	31-Dec-10	CA	514145	Ad Referral	Precision Pet SnooZZy Crate Bed 3000	1	$28
14	25-Jan-11	MI	783323	Luxury Estate	Rabbit Resort Medium Kennel	1	$49
15	17-Feb-11	IN	978034	Ultimate Web Hunter	SnooZZy 1000 Original Fleece Bumper Bed	1	$19

The numerical data items are *Sale Amount* (How much?) and *Quantity* (How many?).

Data types: numerical data items

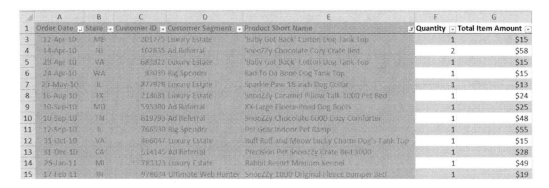

	A	B	C	D	E	F	G
1	Order Date	State	Customer ID	Customer Segment	Product Short Name	Quantity	Total Item Amount
3	12-Apr-10	ME	201775	Luxury Estate	"Baby Got Back" Cotton Dog Tank Top	1	$15
4	14-Apr-10	NJ	102635	Ad Referral	SnooZZy Chocolate Cozy Crate Bed	2	$58
5	23-Apr-10	VA	682822	Luxury Estate	"Baby Got Back" Cotton Dog Tank Top	1	$15
6	24-Apr-10	WA	83039	Big Spender	Bad To Da Bone Dog Tank Top	1	$15
7	23-May-10	IL	877928	Luxury Estate	Sparkle Paw 18-inch Dog Collar	1	$13
8	16-Aug-10	TX	218681	Luxury Estate	SnooZZy Caramel Pillow Talk 1000 Pet Bed	1	$24
9	10-Sep-10	MD	595300	Ad Referral	XX-Large Fleece-lined Dog Boots	1	$25
10	10-Sep-10	TN	619793	Ad Referral	SnooZZy Chocolate 6000 Cozy Comforter	1	$48
11	12-Sep-10	IL	766530	Big Spender	Pet Gear Indoor Pet Ramp	1	$55
12	31-Oct-10	VA	466047	Luxury Estate	Ruff Ruff and Meow Lucky Charm Dog's Tank Top	1	$15
13	31-Dec-10	CA	514145	Ad Referral	Precision Pet SnooZZy Crate Bed 3000	1	$28
14	25-Jan-11	MI	783323	Luxury Estate	Rabbit Resort Medium Kennel	1	$49
15	17-Feb-11	IN	978034	Ultimate Web Hunter	SnooZZy 1000 Original Fleece Bumper Bed	1	$19

Whether categorical or numerical, the names or labels of data items are listed at the top of vertical columns (marked by the letters A, B, C, etc. in the spreadsheet), and each individual transaction is in a horizontal record or row (marked by the numbers 1, 2, 3, etc.).

STEP 2. INVENTORY YOUR DATA: DISCOVER THE DATA SOURCES YOU HAVE AVAILABLE

In God we trust: all others must bring data.

—W. EDWARDS DEMING
American statistician, key to the success of Japan's automakers
in the late 20th century

The next task is to find the right data sources from the pool of data available to you. These sources need to be appropriate for your analysis, since they are crucial in helping you form a final decision at the conclusion of your analysis. There are two types of data sources: company, or **internal,** data sources, and sources from the outside world, or **external,** data sources.

Company or internal data sources: If you've got it, use it

Your Data

You may be very familiar with data to which you have direct access, which is great. However, if you are new to your job, or your company just started collecting new types of data or was acquired by or merged with another company, it is helpful to build an inventory. Even if you know what data you have, you may forget where to find certain data items or other pertinent details if you use them infrequently.

A basic inventory can include a list of datasets (names and short descriptions), the most important data items, data location or how to access the data, and notes on known limitations or flaws in the data. Noting limitations at this point is quite important, both to help you remember them later and to prevent you from accidently presenting results as more accurate than they actually are. You may want to include other information, such as the people responsible for maintaining the dataset, how often the dataset is updated with new data, or shared data items found in multiple datasets (such as *Customer ID* or *Order ID*) in case you would like to link or join them later (explained in *Step 3. Integrate your data*). Organize the inventory alphabetically or in groupings that make sense to you, and if possible, to your colleagues.

Sample Data Item Inventory for Sales Dataset

Transactions
- exported from sales database
- past two years
- does not include returns information, employee purchases

Customers
- exported from customer management system
- current and past as of today

Products
- from product buyers' latest spreadsheet
- all products sold in past two years

Helpful Hint
You don't have to inventory everything all at once.
You can start with the current analysis and continue adding to your inventory as you perform additional analyses. Even if some of the information changes over time, you will have a general idea of where to start and then you can update it as needed.

Colleague or customer data sources

Ask colleagues who work in the area of interest about what data they have or what others may be using. This is similar to what you did in *The First C: Choose Your Questions*, so you may already have this information. Some of the details that may be useful to know include names and locations of the datasets, how they've used the data, known limitations and pitfalls, and how easily the data can be accessed. Add this information to your inventory.

FYI

You may have heard of the term **metadata**.

Metadata are details about a dataset such as who created the dataset, when it was created, and its overall purpose. They also list what's in the dataset, such as the names of tables and columns and the format and length of the data items in the columns. Metadata are usually found in a table or set of tables.

The typical definition given for metadata is "data about data", but this often confuses people because it is ambiguous.

Missing company data sources: Fill in the gaps

If you notice that you are still missing a crucial set of company data or a particular data item, you have three options:

1. Find out if the data exist somewhere that you missed and whether you are able to access them within your time frame.

2. If the set of data doesn't exist, try to find a substitute, or **proxy**, data item or dataset that will work in your analysis, being careful to note how it is different from what you originally planned. For example, if a customer cancelled a subscription service, such as a cell phone plan or cable TV service, a customer survey would be the best way to determine why. But if the customer doesn't reply or you lack the budget for the survey, you can look at recent interactions with the customer, such as complaints or downgraded service.

3. If you can't find a proxy dataset, you may need to find a different approach to your problem, or try to find it outside of your company, if appropriate (we discuss outside or external sources below).

Helpful Hint

You may want to set up a method of collecting the missing data in the future, if you can convince your manager or customer that it is worth the time and money.

Outside or external data sources: Trust but verify

Some types of data that may help you in your analysis can be found outside your company. These are the most common data sources that may be useful for businesspeople, but how useful they actually are to you depends on your particular area or business.

Heads Up
Be careful to avoid data that are ambiguous, from an undocumented source, mislabeled, or misleading. Even if a company or a person has a professional-looking website or tells a persuasive story about how great their datasets are, they still may provide poor-quality data. Don't use data from a suspicious source, unless there is a compelling reason (such as someone needs something done very quickly, you have no other useful information, or you're just trying to prove a point). Just be careful to tell the audience about the dubious nature or limitations of the dataset.

Government data and statistics

Federal governments are great sources for high-quality yet free or inexpensive data covering a wide variety of areas. It will probably take some time to become familiar with the information that can be acquired from various government agencies. Here are a few highlights among many in the U.S. government:

- *U.S. Census Bureau*
  - population growth and demographic information such as ethnicity, family size, marital status, gender, and age
  - invaluable insights into your current or potential customer base
  - publishes *The Statistical Abstract*, the summary of statistics on the social, political, and economic organization of the U.S.
  - runs the *American FactFinder* website

- *Bureau of Labor Statistics in the U. S. Department of Labor*
  - industry and job growth, changes in wages, and comparisons with foreign work forces
  - examples of uses: where to open new branch locations or how wage growth correlates with your sales growth

- *Department of the Treasury*
  - banking data, mortgage rate data, and credit card lending data
  - useful if you sell products that must be financed or are in the financial services area

- *Fedstats*
  - clearinghouse for statistics from over 100 federal agencies
  - search by agency, topic, and geographical region
  - useful if you have a particular area of interest, but are not sure where to start looking

Data Providers

There are many companies that sell consumer information. Some of the traditional "gold standards" are Equifax, Nielsen-Claritas, KBM, Experian, Transunion, Acxiom, and Harte-Hanks. You may want to ask other people at your company if they have experience with a particular data provider or if your company is already a subscriber to one or more of these services.

Online forums

If you have a problem, often there are other analysts out there who either have had the same problem or have a potential solution to yours. Discussion boards, professional forums, and software or product-related forums may be useful, because you can post your problems and read other people's solutions.

Niche areas

Certain businesses or departments may have needs that are specific to their area of specialization. For instance, if you are interested in applying for a grant that funds medical research, you can investigate what types of grants are available and the amounts awarded from specialty providers. To determine your probability of winning a grant or bid, you can find how many applications there have been in the past versus how many applicants won. You may be able to find some of this specialized information on websites for:

- Universities
- Reputable non-profit or non-governmental organizations (NGOs)
- High-quality websites from well-regarded businesses or experts
- Respected media outlets

Helpful Hint

You may need to return to this topic to collect more data, if you later discover that you are missing necessary data or that you selected the wrong data.

Once you have found the data that are relevant to your problem, you will often need to perform a **data download**, which simply means gathering the data into a file or files in a format recognized by the analysis software that you use. Typical formats are Excel, Access, CSV (comma-delimited), TXT (tab-delimited), SAS (a data management, analytics, and statistics package), SPSS (a statistics package), etc. This is also referred to as a **data pull**, **query**, **data extract** or **data dump; data wrangling;** or **pulling a CSV file.** The methods to perform a data download are highly variable depending upon your company, as every system has its own way of exporting data or permitting direct data access. You will need to check with your colleagues or the department that runs the system for details.

Heads Up

If you are working with large datasets, approximately *50,000 rows of data or more*, they can be complex to handle and may take a while to download.

You may want to first:

1. Download a small subset of the data to see if it is what you need. For example, instead of pulling the whole two years, download just one month.
2. Read the next section, *Step 3. Integrate your data.* If it applies to your situation, you will likely save yourself some time.

Helpful Hint

Business and IT *can* get along!

Businesspeople often tell us that it's difficult to get the right data from IT (the information technology or business information systems department). To paraphrase the most common sentiment, "It's like they're speaking a different language". For ideas on how to improve the relationship between business and IT, we asked a number of IT people about the challenges they face.

The most cited issue? Businesspeople asking for data without specifying what their analysis questions are or what they are planning to do with the data. This frequently causes IT to pull the wrong data, which in turn leads to more work and frustration for both parties.

To cut down on wasted time, the most successful model that we've encountered is the replacement of the traditional system where data requests are made through a supervisor with one where IT professionals are directly partnered with businesspeople to collaborate on projects.

We've asked IT people how this arrangement works for them. One person effectively summed up the overall response: "It felt weird at first, but now I really like it. Everyone wants to be part of a team that's successful."

STEP 3. INTEGRATE YOUR DATA: MERGE MULTIPLE DATASETS

To err is human,
but to really foul things up requires a computer.

—1978 FARMERS' ALMANAC

It isn't uncommon for the data that you need to be found in multiple datasets, for instance in both a sales database and a customer database. Yet it is much easier to analyze data in most software programs if the data are combined in one dataset.

Perhaps you've already dealt with this issue "manually" by copying and pasting data from one spreadsheet into another. If you have, this can be nerve-racking, as you are never quite sure if all the data you need wind up in the right place in the final spreadsheet. Also, manually merging or combining your data isn't feasible for large datasets. There are much better ways to leverage your analysis software to combine multiple datasets, and here we will discuss the two most common methods: **unions** and **joins**.

Union:
Combine or append two or more datasets
that contain the same data items

If you have multiple datasets that contain the same data items, you should perform a **union** to combine them into one dataset. This is also referred to as **stacking**, **appending** or **setting** the data. For instance, you may have customers from the East, West and South in three separate data files, and it would be easier to analyze them all at once. A second example is that you have two sales datasets, one with data from January, February and March, and one from April, May and June, so you combine them into a single dataset that contains all six months, January through June. This is shown in the illustration.

Union Example:
Combine datasets with the same data items
The two sheets on top each contain three months of sales data
The bottom sheet has all six months of data combined

	A	B	C
1	Order Month	Customer Segment	Sales
2	Jan-10	Ad Referral	$92,172
3	Jan-10	Big Spender	$10,256
4	Jan-10	Luxury Estate	$25,006
5	Jan-10	Ultimate Web Hunter	$16,891
6	Feb-10	Ad Referral	$61,514

	A	B	C
1	Order Month	Customer Segment	Sales
2	Apr-10	Ad Referral	$217,983
3	Apr-10	Big Spender	$32,515
4	Apr-10	Luxury Estate	$71,812
5	Apr-10	Ultimate Web Hunter	$49,718
6	May-10	Ad Referral	$246,161

	A	B	C
1	Order Month	Customer Segment	Sales
2	Jan-10	Ad Referral	$92,172
3	Feb-10	Ad Referral	$61,514
4	Mar-10	Ad Referral	$67,931
5	Apr-10	Ad Referral	$217,983
6	May-10	Ad Referral	$246,161
7	Jun-10	Ad Referral	$92,377
8	Jan-10	Big Spender	$10,256
9	Feb-10	Big Spender	$12,831
10	Mar-10	Big Spender	$7,690
11	Apr-10	Big Spender	$32,515
12	May-10	Big Spender	$37,362
13	Jun-10	Big Spender	$8,577
14	Jan-10	Luxury Estate	$25,006

Now all six months of data can be analyzed at one time.

Helpful Hint

For a quick check to verify that the union worked, ensure that you have *more* records or rows in the final dataset than in either alone.

If you have time, you can add up the rows from the two datasets to determine the exact amount that you should have.

Join:
Combine two or more datasets based on matching values in at least one data item

If you're lucky, all the data items that you need to answer your questions will be found in one dataset. However, they often will be in two or more datasets. The best way to execute your analysis is to combine these into a single new dataset.

Joining is the technique to save time and your sanity. As long as each dataset contains one or more data items (columns) in common, you can join them. Joining also is called **merging**, **consolidating** or **data blending**. The common data items found in each dataset are called **keys**, since they are used to match the records in each dataset with each other.

An example is having one dataset with sales data and a second dataset with demographic data (such as population per state). Both datasets contain the state abbreviation, which would be the key data item in this case. You can join these two into a third, new dataset using the state abbreviation field.

The most common type of join, called an **inner join**, results in a new dataset that comprises all rows from each of the two original datasets that have a *matching* state abbreviation value in both datasets.

Heads Up

In most software tools, an *inner join* type is the default behavior when you use the join feature or function.

Inner joins will only keep records from the data at hand if there is a *matching value based on the key* in both datasets.

All other records are ignored and NOT added to the resulting dataset.

Inner join is the typical join type:
Combine datasets with at least one data item in common
Keys are Year and State, found in both the left and right tables

	A	B	C
1	Year	State	Sales
2	2010	AZ	$62,210
3	2010	CA	$324,803
4	2010	CT	$39,365
5	2010	NC	$28,487
6	2010	WA	$11,571
7	2011	AZ	$122,987
8	2011	CA	$632,325
9	2011	CT	$78,758
10	2011	NC	$32,502
11	2011	WA	$16,877

	A	B	C
1	Year	State	Population
2	2010	AZ	6,595,778
3	2010	CA	36,961,664
4	2010	CT	3,518,288
5	2010	MI	9,883,640
6	2010	WA	6,664,195
7	2011	AZ	6,661,735
8	2011	CA	37,700,897
9	2011	CT	3,511,251
10	2011	MI	9,876,187
11	2011	WA	6,830,799

59

Joined dataset contains both sales and population data only for years and states found in both the left and right tables
There's also a new metric calculated using Sales and Population

	A	B	C	D	E
1	Year	State	Sales	Population	Sales per hundred people
2	2010	AZ	$62,210	6,595,778	$0.94
3	2011	AZ	$122,987	6,661,735	$1.85
4	2010	CA	$324,803	36,961,664	$0.88
5	2011	CA	$632,325	37,700,897	$1.68
6	2010	CT	$39,365	3,518,288	$1.12
7	2011	CT	$78,758	3,511,251	$2.24
8	2010	WA	$11,571	6,664,195	$0.17
9	2011	WA	$16,877	6,830,799	$0.25

For both 2010 and 2011, note that North Carolina (NC) is in the left table, and Michigan (MI) is in the right table, but neither are in the joined dataset. To be included, a state must be in both the left and right datasets. Also, by joining the sales and population data in one sheet, sales per hundred people can be calculated, as shown in the final spreadsheet.

To check if the inner join worked, the final dataset will contain:

- *At most* the smallest number of records or rows found in either of the two original datasets

Helpful Hint
For another quick check to see if any join type worked, the final dataset will usually have *more* data items (columns) than in either dataset alone.

You may require more advanced joins for your analysis. These usually will be **left joins**, but also could be **right joins** or **outer joins**.

A **left join** results in a new table with all the rows from the left table, and the rows from the right table that have matching values for the keys. "Left" refers to the order that you specify the tables in your data analysis software, but the details on how to join tables differ depending on what application you are using.

**Left join: all rows from the original left table,
plus rows from the right table with matching key values**
*Inner join rows in light gray text, with additional rows bolded
(NC data from 2010 and 2011)*

	A	B	C	D	E
1	Year	State	Sales	Population	Sales per hundred people
2	2010	AZ	$62,210	6,595,778	$0.94
3	2011	AZ	$122,987	6,661,735	$1.85
4	2010	CA	$324,803	36,961,664	$0.88
5	2011	CA	$632,325	37,700,897	$1.68
6	2010	CT	$39,365	3,518,288	$1.12
7	2011	CT	$78,758	3,511,251	$2.24
8	**2010**	**NC**	**$28,487**		
9	**2011**	**NC**	**$32,502**		
10	2010	WA	$11,571	6,664,195	$0.17
11	2011	WA	$16,877	6,830,799	$0.25

The final dataset in a left join will contain:

- *At least* the number of rows in the left table

- But possibly more
    - Can occur when there are duplicate matching rows (based on the key fields) in the right table
    - Note that this is not demonstrated in the illustration

A **right join** is the reverse of a left join; it results in a new table with all the rows from the right table, and the rows from the left table that have matching values for the keys.

Right join: reverse of the left join
All rows from right table plus matching rows in left
Inner join rows in light gray text, with additional rows bolded
(MI data from 2010 and 2011)

	A	B	C	D	E
1	Year	State	Sales	Population	Sales per hundred people
2	2010	AZ	$62,210	6,595,778	$0.94
3	2011	AZ	$122,987	6,661,735	$1.85
4	2010	CA	$324,803	36,961,664	$0.88
5	2011	CA	$632,325	37,700,897	$1.68
6	2010	CT	$39,365	3,518,288	$1.12
7	2011	CT	$78,758	3,511,251	$2.24
8	**2010**	**MI**		**9,883,640**	
9	**2011**	**MI**		**9,876,187**	
10	2010	WA	$11,571	6,664,195	$0.17
11	2011	WA	$16,877	6,830,799	$0.25

The final dataset in a right join will contain:

- *At least* the number of rows in the right table

- But possibly more (as explained in the left join)

An **outer join** results in a new table with all of the rows from both the left and right tables, whether or not they contain matching values for the keys.

Outer join: all rows from both left and right tables
Inner join rows in light gray text, with additional rows bolded
(Both NC and MI data from 2010 and 2011)

	A	B	C	D	E
1	Year	State	Sales	Population	Sales per hundred people
2	2010	AZ	$62,210	6,595,778	$0.94
3	2011	AZ	$122,987	6,661,735	$1.85
4	2010	CA	$324,803	36,961,664	$0.88
5	2011	CA	$632,325	37,700,897	$1.68
6	2010	CT	$39,365	3,518,288	$1.12
7	2011	CT	$78,758	3,511,251	$2.24
8	***2010***	**MI**		**9,883,640**	
9	***2011***	**MI**		**9,876,187**	
10	***2010***	**NC**	**$28,487**		
11	***2011***	**NC**	**$32,502**		
12	2010	WA	$11,571	6,664,195	$0.17
13	2011	WA	$16,877	6,830,799	$0.25

The final dataset in an outer join will contain:

- *At least* the number of rows in the larger of the two tables, which occurs when all rows in the smaller table match those in the bigger table

- *At most* the number of rows found in the two tables combined, which occurs when there are NO matches between the two tables

- Typically, you'll have a row count somewhere in between these two values

RECAP OF THE SECOND C: COLLECT YOUR DATA

- To take control of your data, first you have to collect the right data for your question and organize it in one place.

- The three steps of collecting your data are:

  - Identify your data

  - Inventory your data

  - Integrate your data

- You can identify your data as one of two main types: **categorical** or **numerical**.

- Create a **data inventory** by utilizing internal, or company, data sources and external, or outside, data sources.

- Integrate different datasets into one dataset with a **union** or **join**.

Now that you have collected your data, you are ready to move on to *The Third C: Check Out Your Data*, to see what basic information you can compile about your data to begin to answer some of your business questions.

THE THIRD C:
CHECK OUT YOUR DATA

One of the effects of living with electric information
is that we live habitually in a state of information overload.
There's always more than you can cope with.

—MARSHALL MCLUHAN (1967)
Pioneer of the study of popular culture

Now that you have accomplished the difficult task of collecting your data, you can check out your data. In this C, you'll begin to obtain actionable insights to help you and others make better decisions about your business, because you'll be reviewing information about important data items.

To do this, you'll use a set of six techniques that we call *the data review toolkit*. This toolkit will help you to become familiar with your dataset and to answer essential questions about key data items. In the least, you'll confirm what you already knew about the data. However, your results may contradict what you or colleagues thought. If you are lucky, you will discover answers for questions that were driving the analysis in the first place.

Below we've developed a road map of how to use the data review toolkit. Each tool won't apply to every dataset. After you become familiar with the tools, you will have an idea of which ones are useful, depending both on the data you have and what questions you are asking. Later in the book, we will use most of these tools for more complex analysis. Note that you can use these tools with any data analysis package, such as Excel, SAS, SPSS, or Tableau Software, but these examples are not tied to any particular software.

For your quick reference later, we suggest keeping a short list of your results for each tool in a Word document, spreadsheet, or checklist. This list is also useful in case someone asks for basic information about the dataset, so that you can provide answers quickly.

Helpful Hint

It may be helpful to also read *The Fourth C: Clean Up Your Data* before you start your basic data review.

You may want to review your data and clean them up at the same time, as soon as problems pop up.

Here is a road map of the data review toolkit that we'll cover in this C. A more detailed table for your reference is included in the recap at the end.

THE DATA REVIEW TOOLKIT

#1.   Sort

#2.   Filter

#3.   Summary values
- Sum
- Count
- Maximum and Minimum
- Span
- Average

#4.   Ranking
- Median
- Percentiles

#5.   Change over time

#6.   Reality checks
- Internal checks
- External checks

Bonus. Protect your assets

TOOL #1. SORT: REORDER YOUR DATA

The first line of attack in a basic data review is to **sort** your data. If you would like your data listed or displayed in the order of a particular data item (whether categorical or numerical), you can use sorting to reorder the dataset. Sorting can be useful in verifying that you've downloaded the right data and is a good starting point for finding simple answers to your business questions.

If you are checking out your data pull, sorting is good for datasets with a relatively small numbers of records. Sorting is also useful if you have a wide range of values or missing values for numerical data items. For example, sales transactions can have many different dollar amounts depending on what combinations of items were purchased, so you can sort to look at the highest and lowest amounts to see if the data match with your prior information about the dataset.

Throughout this book, techniques will be demonstrated using data from a large pet product company. In this illustration, we've pulled customer transaction data and we want to find out which customer has spent the most in a single transaction.

Not very useful to find the best sale!
Original order of data when opened (by transaction date)

Transaction Date	State	Customer ID	Customer Segment	Product Short Name	Quantity	Transaction Amount
10-Feb-10	ID	236640	Ultimate Web Hunter	Stinky Pet Tee	1	$15
12-Apr-10	ME	201775	Luxury Estate	'Baby Got Back' Cotton Dog Tank Top	1	$15
23-Apr-10	VA	683822	Luxury Estate	'Baby Got Back' Cotton Dog Tank Top	1	$15
24-Apr-10	WA	83039	Big Spender	Bad To Da Bone Dog Tank Top	1	$15
23-May-10	IL	877928	Luxury Estate	Sparkle Paw 18-inch Dog Collar	1	$13
16-Aug-10	TX	218681	Luxury Estate	SnooZZy Caramel Pillow Talk 1000 Pet Bed	1	$24
10-Sep-10	MD	595300	Ad Referral	XX-Large Fleece-lined Dog Boots	1	$25
31-Oct-10	VA	466047	Luxury Estate	Ruff Ruff and Meow Lucky Charm Dog's Tank Top	1	$15
31-Dec-10	CA	514145	Ad Referral	Precision Pet SnooZZy Crate Bed 3000	1	$28
25-Jan-11	MI	783323	Luxury Estate	Rabbit Resort Medium Kennel	1	$49
23-Sep-11	CA	223626	Ad Referral	Ruff Ruff and Meow Lucky Charm Dog's Tank Top	1	$15
10-Nov-11	CA	159776	Big Spender	'Baby Got Back' Cotton Dog Tank Top	1	$15
10-Nov-11	CO	461814	Ad Referral	Rabbit Resort Medium Kennel	1	$49

However, our data are listed in the spreadsheet by the transaction date, so we sort by highest transaction amount.

Our best sale is $480
Sorted to find highest transaction amount

Transaction Date	State	Customer ID	Customer Segment	Product Short Name	Quantity	Transaction Amount
4-Dec-11	DC	302500	Big Spender	Large Burgundy Microfiber Memory Foam Bed	8	$480
30-Oct-11	FL	412848	Luxury Estate	Sorority Hoodie Medium Dog Dress	9	$207
22-Sep-11	CA	473408	Big Spender	Large Chocolate Microfiber Memory Foam Bed	1	$60
24-Nov-11	FL	291257	Ultimate Web Hunter	Large Burgundy Microfiber Memory Foam Bed	1	$60
24-Oct-11	FL	738069	Luxury Estate	Large Chocolate Microfiber Memory Foam Bed	1	$60
11-Dec-11	TX	969043	Big Spender	Majestic Pet Bagel-style Burgundy 40-inch Dog Bed	1	$60
14-Apr-10	NJ	102635	Ad Referral	SnooZZy Chocolate Cozy Crate Bed	2	$58
16-Oct-11	TX	732489	Ad Referral	SnooZZy Chocolate Cozy Crate Bed 6000 (51 x 33)	1	$56
11-Nov-11	WI	139004	Ad Referral	SnooZZy Chocolate Cozy Crate Bed 6000 (51 x 33)	1	$56

Beyond simple sorting by just one column, it can be particularly useful to do a *multi-sort* or *nested sort*. This is when you sort the entire dataset by a data item, and then sort again by a second data item. For instance, once we sorted by transaction amount, we decided it would be informative to sort *first* by state and *then* by transaction amount. This allowed us to spot the largest transaction for each state, as shown in the illustration.

Our best sale is our only sale in Washington D.C.
A nested sort:
first sort by state, then sort by transaction amount

Transaction Date	State	Customer ID	Customer Segment	Product Short Name	Quantity	Transaction Amount
22-Sep-11	CA	473408	Big Spender	Large Chocolate Microfiber Memory Foam Bed	1	$60
31-Dec-10	CA	514145	Ad Referral	Precision Pet SnooZZy Crate Bed 3000	1	$28
10-Nov-11	CA	159776	Big Spender	'Baby Got Back' Cotton Dog Tank Top	1	$15
23-Sep-11	CA	223626	Ad Referral	Ruff Ruff and Meow Lucky Charm Dog's Tank Top	1	$15
10-Nov-11	CO	461814	Ad Referral	Rabbit Resort Medium Kennel	1	$49
4-Dec-11	DC	302500	Big Spender	Large Burgundy Microfiber Memory Foam Bed	8	$480
30-Oct-11	FL	412848	Luxury Estate	Sorority Hoodie Medium Dog Dress	9	$207
24-Nov-11	FL	291257	Ultimate Web Hunter	Large Burgundy Microfiber Memory Foam Bed	1	$60
24-Oct-11	FL	738069	Luxury Estate	Large Chocolate Microfiber Memory Foam Bed	1	$60

TOOL #2. FILTER: FOCUS ON THE RIGHT DATA

Although frequently overlooked, **filters** are one of the most powerful tools for basic data review, and are typically very quick in most software applications. If you would like to select or exclude particular values of either a categorical or numerical data item, such as a certain product, location, region, customer, date, or sales amount, filters are the way to go. Similar to sorting, filters allow you to review your data pull and begin asking simple yet important questions about your data pull.

When you have a dataset with many rows or columns, filters can be useful to verify that that you have the right data or that you're not missing data. If you know the range of values that you should have pulled, then you can use a filter to rapidly see if it falls within the range. For example, if you have retail stores in 10 states, but filtering by state shows just 8 states in your data pull, you're likely missing data. Also, if you requested data from the last 6 months, but filtering by month shows that there are 12 months, you have unwanted months included in your dataset. The illustration shows a filter dialog box that's missing a couple of months.

Where's March and August?
No sales in these months—or should we be suspicious of the data?

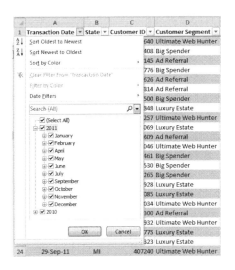

Other examples include filtering to show only your top 25 customers by profit, selecting sales dates for a particular product, sales on Monday or Tuesday only, profit in the previous quarter versus the same period last year, or sales transactions larger than $100. The illustration shows a filter that displays only sales of dog tank tops.

Want to look at one type of product?
Filter to display only "Dog Tank Top" transactions

	Transaction Date	State	Customer ID	Customer Segment	Product Short Name	Quantity	Transaction Amount
5	10-Nov-11	CA	159776	Big Spender	'Baby Got Back' Cotton Dog Tank Top	1	$15
6	23-Sep-11	CA	223626	Ad Referral	Ruff Ruff and Meow Lucky Charm Dog's Tank Top	1	$15
21	20-Jul-11	ME	466932	Ultimate Web Hunter	'Spoiled Rotten' Cotton Dog Tank Top	1	$18
22	12-Apr-10	ME	201775	Luxury Estate	'Baby Got Back' Cotton Dog Tank Top	1	$15
25	17-Apr-11	MN	362793	Luxury Estate	'Spoiled Rotten' Cotton Dog Tank Top	1	$18
30	31-Oct-11	OR	123780	Big Spender	'Spoiled Rotten' Cotton Dog Tank Top	1	$18
32	7-May-11	TN	930457	Big Spender	'I Love Matzah Balls' Cotton Dog Tank Top	1	$17
36	23-Apr-10	VA	683822	Luxury Estate	'Baby Got Back' Cotton Dog Tank Top	1	$15
37	31-Oct-10	VA	466047	Luxury Estate	Ruff Ruff and Meow Lucky Charm Dog's Tank Top	1	$15
43	24-Apr-10	WA	83039	Big Spender	Bad To Da Bone Dog Tank Top	1	$15
44	29-Nov-11	WA	764675	Ad Referral	'Ho! Ho! Ho!' Dog Tank Top	1	$15

Similar to nested or multi-sorts, you can apply *multiple* or *cascading filters* to isolate a very specific subset of data, such as sales transactions larger than $100 that were placed on Mondays or Tuesdays. In this illustration we applied multiple filters to dog tank top sales.

Great for very specific questions
Multiple filters: "Dog Tank Top" → 2011 Transactions → State → Big Spender and Luxury Estate customers

	Transaction Date	State	Customer ID	Customer Segment	Product Short Name	Quantity	Transaction Amount
5	10-Nov-11	CA	159776	Big Spender	'Baby Got Back' Cotton Dog Tank Top	1	$15
25	17-Apr-11	MN	362793	Luxury Estate	'Spoiled Rotten' Cotton Dog Tank Top	1	$18
30	31-Oct-11	OR	123780	Big Spender	'Spoiled Rotten' Cotton Dog Tank Top	1	$18
32	7-May-11	TN	930457	Big Spender	'I Love Matzah Balls' Cotton Dog Tank Top	1	$17

Helpful Hint

If your dataset has a large number of columns, or you are not using some of them, hide the extra columns.

This will reduce confusion for you and anyone else using the data pull. Most software analysis tools have hide and unhide functions, typically accessed by right-clicking on the column header and selecting hide or unhide.

TOOL #3. SUMMARY VALUES: CONDENSE YOUR DATA ITEMS FOR SIMPLICITY

You can condense multiple individual values (rows or records) of a data item into a **summary value**. Summary values are also called **aggregates**, **aggregations**, **groupings**, or **summary statistics**. They are helpful in painting a general picture of the overall "shape" of a data item, rather than focusing on individual values. For instance, you can find out what a typical customer spends on a single shopping trip, which days last year had the highest total sales, and how much more your top customers spend compared to your bottom customers. There are many types of summary values, but for brevity we'll discuss just a few that are useful for reviewing your data: **sum**, **count**, **maximums** and **minimums**, **span**, and **average**.

Helpful Hint
If you have a large dataset, a useful trick is to start with either a subset or a random sample of your dataset.
Large datasets (more than 50,000 records) may be confusing for you to handle until you are more familiar with the data items. They can also take a long time for the software to process. You may choose to select a 1% or even a 10% random sample for quick review (for example, Excel has a random sample function). A one-million row dataset is much more manageable if you look at 10,000 or 100,000 rows first.

Sum: Add up your data values

There is a good chance that you have already utilized the most common summary value, **sum** (also called **addition** or **total**), because everyone wants to know "How much?": "How much were our sales last week?" or "How much did we spend on marketing last year?" or "How much time am I spending on customer service calls during the day?". It's a good idea to walk into meetings knowing at least "how much" for the most important numerical data items or metrics.

This illustration shows the sum of transaction amounts filtered by customer type or segment.

Big Spenders are our big spenders
Sum of sales, by customer type, sorted from highest to lowest

Customer Segment	Sum of Transaction Amount
Big Spender	$ 858
Ad Referral	$ 470
Luxury Estate	$ 428
Ultimate Web Hunter	$ 211
Grand Total	**$ 1,967**

What are our best states and products?
Sum of sales transactions, by state and product, sorted from highest to lowest

Product Short Name	Sum of Transaction Amount
⊟ DC	$ 480
Large Burgundy Microfiber Memory Foam Bed	$ 480
⊟ FL	$ 327
Sorority Hoodie Medium Dog Dress	$ 207
Large Burgundy Microfiber Memory Foam Bed	$ 60
Large Chocolate Microfiber Memory Foam Bed	$ 60
⊟ WA	$ 147
Petmate Fresh Flow Pet Fountain Fresh Flow Pet	$ 35
SnooZZy Chocolate 2000 Cozy Comforter	$ 24
Doggie Dental Fresh/ Shed-X Hair Pet Care Set	$ 22
Small/ Medium Zebra Print Dog Sundress	$ 19
Outward Hound Blue Designer Rain Jacket	$ 17
'Ho! Ho! Ho!' Dog Tank Top	$ 15
Bad To Da Bone Dog Tank Top	$ 15

Helpful Hint

It may be helpful to sort your data after filtering, counting, etc. to make it quicker and easier to get information.

Heads Up

Remember that numerical data items typically can be summed, but categorical items can't be—even if they contain numbers.

Count: How many do you have?

For data items that can be counted, you may want to find out how many of each type there are, which is called a **count.** Counts are usually done with categorical data items, which is different from the other summary values listed here. Examples are the number of customers who bought luxury pet beds, how many products you have in your inventory, and the number of sales transactions.

The illustration shows the counts of products sold for each product line.

Which product lines have the most products?
Count of number of products sold within each product line, sorted from highest to lowest count

Product Line	Count of Products
Pet Beds	251
Pet Apparel	180
Collars, Harnesses & Leashes	160
Pet Toys	87
Crates & Kennels	66
Animal Feeders & Waterers	65
Cat Supplies	64
Pet Gates & Pet Doors	61
Pet Travel	49
Pet Treats	37

Maximum and Minimum: The highs and the lows of your data

Looking at the **maximum (max)** or **minimum (min)** values for various numerical data items or metrics of interest is often enlightening. Are these summary values what you expect? For example, you may want to know the highest (maximum) purchase amount last month for a single customer, or which customer service agent answered the fewest (minimum) phone calls.

In this illustration, we were looking for the product lines with the most and least expensive products.

What are our least and most expensive products?
Minimum and maximum selling price
within each product line, sorted by maximum

Product Line	Min	Max
Pet Fish & Reptile Supplies	$ 43.99	$ 1,299.99
Bird Supplies	$ 8.29	$ 499.99
Collars, Harnesses & Leashes	$ 3.99	$ 379.95
Pet Gates & Pet Doors	$ 14.99	$ 319.95
Pet Beds	$ 17.39	$ 267.99
Crates & Kennels	$ 18.99	$ 258.48
Cat Supplies	$ 7.99	$ 179.99
Pet Grooming	$ 6.29	$ 146.99
Pet Houses	$ 19.49	$ 138.99

Heads Up

Max and min values may be somewhat misleading, since they can occur only once in your data and/or be very far from the next closest value.

Values that are very different from the bulk of the data are called **outliers**, because they are the extreme values rather than the typical ones. Outliers are often useful for extremely specific purposes, such as fraud analysis, audits, and customer profiling.

Span: The ranges of values in your data

How far apart are your max and min? For instance, if your highest-priced item is $100, and your lowest is $5, the **span**, **range**, or **spread** of your data is $95. Like max and min, span applies to metrics, or numerical data items. You also may want to know how much more the max is than the min. In that case, you might simply divide the max by the min.

For instance, you are selling pet beds, and you need to know how much more expensive your highest-price bed is relative to your lowest-price bed. Divide $100 (the max) by $5 (the min). This equals 20, so the most expensive bed is 20 times the cost of the least expensive bed.

Heads Up

Like the max and min, the span may be misleading, as extreme maxes and mins can cause the span to extend much farther than the bulk of the data values.

Average: Typical values for your data items

Find the **average** (also called the **mean**) value for numerical data items that you are focusing on, which is often thought of as the "typical" or representative value. You may be interested in metrics such as average sale amount, average product price, or average count of customers on a particular day, week, or month.

Technically, the average is the sum of all the values for a data item, divided by the count of how many values are included in the average.

If you sold 5 pet beds, at prices of $20, $10, $10, $10, and $5, the average is $20+$10+$10+$10+$5 (which totals $55) divided by the 5 pet beds sold.

So, $55 / 5 pet beds equals an average of $11 per pet bed.

In addition to average, the illustration shows other summary values.

Looking for details to quickly compare various product lines?
Summary values for product line price data:
minimum, maximum, span, and average

Product Line	Min	Max	Span	Average
Pet Fish & Reptile Supplies	$ 43.99	$ 1,299.99	$ 1,256.00	$ 379.41
Bird Supplies	$ 8.29	$ 499.99	$ 491.70	$ 109.81
Collars, Harnesses & Leashes	$ 3.99	$ 379.95	$ 375.96	$ 35.09
Pet Gates & Pet Doors	$ 14.99	$ 319.95	$ 304.96	$ 72.35
Pet Beds	$ 17.39	$ 267.99	$ 250.60	$ 44.50
Crates & Kennels	$ 18.99	$ 258.48	$ 239.49	$ 85.64
Cat Supplies	$ 7.99	$ 179.99	$ 172.00	$ 92.86
Pet Grooming	$ 6.29	$ 146.99	$ 140.70	$ 20.93
Pet Houses	$ 19.49	$ 138.99	$ 119.50	$ 88.69

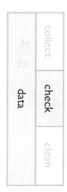

FYI

There is a joke among statisticians that goes:

A statistician can have his head in an oven and his feet in ice,
and he will say that on average he feels fine.

The take-home message is that the average value of a data item may not exist. For example, the average cost of the pet beds you've sold may be $50. However, you only sell $100 and $5 pet beds—no one actually bought a pet bed for $50.

Heads Up

Average can be greatly affected by just a few outliers, which may "pull" the average much higher or lower than if the outlier weren't included.

For instance, if the average income in your neighborhood is $50,000, and Bill Gates moved in next door, the average would skyrocket because of just one person.

TOOL #4. RANKING:
ARRANGE DATA FROM TOP TO BOTTOM

As we mentioned in the alerts above, sometimes max, min, span, and average don't provide accurate pictures of most of the data. Instead, **ranking** the individual data values can help overcome some of these shortcomings. **Median** and **percentiles** are data review tools that can rank data.

Median: Half are above, half are below

The **median** is the data value or values right in the middle of your span of values for a particular numerical data item.

For example, what is the median cost of the pet collars you sold yesterday?

You sold 5 pet collars for $10, $7, $6, $3 and $2. The middle value is $6, which is the median for an odd number of pet collars.

If you have an even number of pet collars, selling for $10, $7, $6, $5, $3, and $2, then your median is the average of the two middle values: $5.50.

Although it is similar to an average, the median will often give you different information than the average.

Here's an example. Your average customer spent $50,000 last year on the software that you sell. You have two groups of customers: a lot of small businesses that spent $500-$1000, and a few large companies that spent $100,000. The median is only $900, much less than the $50,000 average, and describes the bulk of your customers (in count, not in sales amounts) more accurately.

The illustration compares median and average using product prices for each product line. Note that Pet Fish & Reptile Supplies contains an outlier, and that the average is quite a bit higher than the median (partially due to the outlier).

What's the difference between the median and average summary values by product line?
Each circle is a product sold within the product line

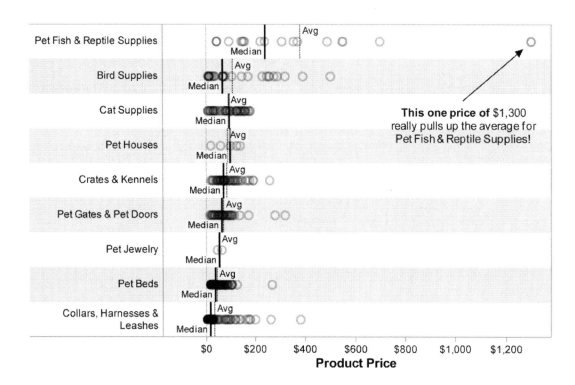

This one price of $1,300 really pulls up the average for Pet Fish & Reptile Supplies!

FYI

If there are many data points that represent either high or low values relative to the bulk of the data, then the median and the average are going to be quite different from each other.

The median is a type of **percentile**, covered in the next bullet point.

Percentiles: Divide your data up into equal parts

Dividing your data into **percentiles** provides more details than looking only at the median. Choose your numerical data item or metric of importance. Rank all your records from lowest to highest by sorting based on that metric, then count the number of records and divide by 100.

For example, if you sort according to sales by customer, and you have 5000 customers, 5000 divided by 100 equals 50.

The top 50 customers in sale amounts make up the last or top percentile. Each additional percentile includes 50 more customers.

The last or top **decile** (the root "dec" means "10") contains the top 500 customers (50 customers X 10 percentiles).

Deciles are the 1st (0%-10%), 2nd (10%-20%), 3rd (20%-30%), etc., up to the 10th decile (90%-100%).

The terms "0th percentile" and "100th percentile" typically aren't used, though—they are simply called the **min** and the **max,** respectively (discussed in *Tool #3*).

Quartiles are separated at the 25th, 50th and 75th percentiles. The cutoff at 50% is the **median**.

The illustrations contrast average and span with the 25th and 75th percentiles.

**Prices of products (circles) within each product line:
Average (solid line) and span (grey background) <u>versus</u>...**

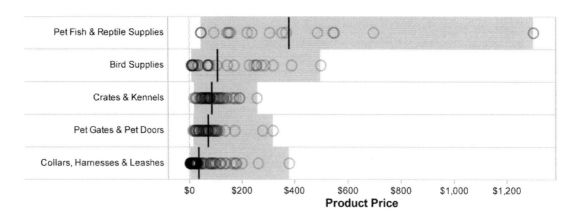

**Median (dotted line), average (solid line) and
25th to 75th percentiles (grey background)**
*Note the average and median for Pet Fish & Reptile Supplies
(the average is "pulled up" by the extreme maximum value)*

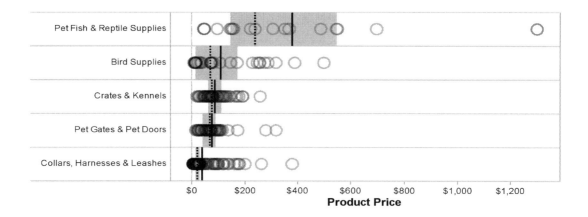

You may ask "Why are we comparing these two graphs?" People usually use average, minimum and maximum to describe their data. Remember that these values can be skewed a lot by a few extreme data points. Median and percentiles aren't affected by extreme values, so they often give you more information about your typical transaction or record. Using the 25th and 75th percentiles in particular identifies half of all your transactions, the most common ones "in the middle".

Helpful Hint

Because median and percentiles are less affected by outliers, they are useful if you are planning how to manage your business in the future.

For instance, if your average sale amount is cut in half, that may be due to a few extreme low values. But if your median drops to half, you should really be worried—time to make some serious changes.

Another example of how percentiles are useful is in finding your top or bottom 1% of transactions (the extreme values) as we show in the following illustration. The top 1% is also referred to as the 99th percentile, and the bottom 1% is the 1st percentile.

Transaction amounts within each product line:
Bottom 1% (outside grey area to the left)
Median (dotted line)
Top 1% or 99th percentile (outside grey area to the right)

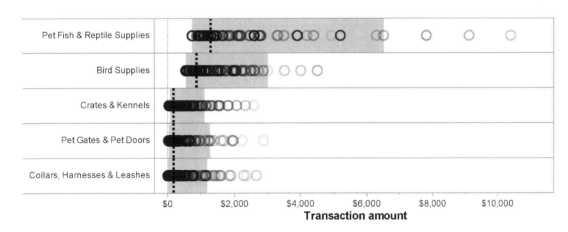

Helpful Hint

Commonly used percentiles in presentations are the median, 99th and 1st percentiles (top or bottom 1%), 25th and 75th percentiles, and deciles (1st, 2nd, 3rd and so on).

FYI

You may hear the term **distribution** in regards to data.

Although it has a technical definition in the field of statistics, the meaning useful to accidental analysts is that for a particular data item, a distribution can tell you where to find the:

- *bulk of values*, typically between the 10th and 90th percentiles, shown here in black
- *extreme values*, usually in the 10th and 90th or 1st and 99th percentiles, shown here in grey

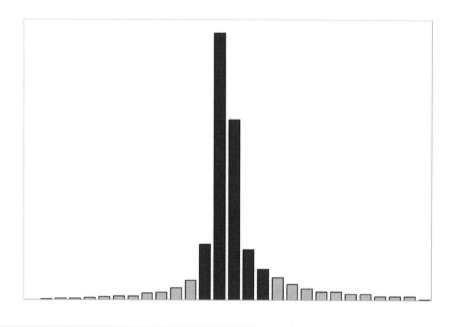

TOOL #5. CHANGE OVER TIME:
SHOW HOW YOUR DATA FLUCTUATE OR VARY

How your data **change over time** (also called a **time series**) is essential to any type of business. Depending on what you are interested in, you can look at what has occurred over minutes, hours, days, weeks, months, quarters, years, decades, or even seasons. Although you can look at this in a spreadsheet, it is far easier to understand change over time in a graph. Graphs show the differences between time periods quite clearly and may make apparent patterns that repeat themselves.

Examples include a time series of marketing spending for online versus print for the last three months, or call volume to your customer service center during every minute over the last eight hours. The illustration shows sales for Q1 and Q2 over the last two years.

Great for seeing the overall pattern and for finding unusual values
Sales by month for the first half of 2010 versus 2011

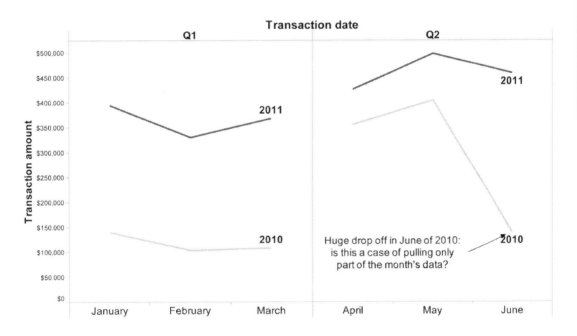

TOOL #6. REALITY CHECKS: CONSIDER DATA IN THE CONTEXT OF YOUR BUSINESS

*Everybody gets so much information all day long
that they lose their common sense.*

—GERTRUDE STEIN
American writer and art collector

Sometimes you can get so caught up in doing things with your data, you might not think about what your initial review results actually mean. When performing your basic data review, it is a great idea to consider if the numbers "make sense". There are several ways to apply this tool.

Internal checks: Use company information as a benchmark

Compare your results from the other tools to common information that you have about what's going on within your company. If you know that your company sold 100 yachts last year over twelve months, and your data review shows that in November you sold 98 yachts, there probably is a problem. If the results look good on the surface, you may want to compare your results to other information you have access to. For example, if you are preparing your annual report, compare it to your recent quarterly reports and last year's annual report.

In a prior analysis, the Carolina Plush Chenille bed was our top seller in *Pet Beds*—look at the illustration to see if it is the same. Is something missing in this new data download, or did we get an entirely wrong set of data?

Highlighting a problem to investigate:
Our top seller is different than the one found during previous analysis

	A	B
1	**Product Line**	**Sum**
2	⊟Pet Beds	$ 11,168.86
3	All-weather Cushioned Resin Wicker Dog Bed	$ 267.99
4	Carolina Plush Chenile 50-inch Bolster Bed	$ 209.98
5	Carolina Plush Chenile 42-inch Bolster Bed	$ 172.98
6	Tufted Hearth Paisley Microfiber Large Pet Bed	$ 159.97
7	Carolina Plush Chenille 35-inch Bolster Pet Bed	$ 128.98
8	XL Orthopedic Memory Foam Dog Bed (36 in x 52 in)	$ 125.99
9	Petmate Deluxe Double Orthopedic Pet Bed	$ 123.98
10	Majestic Pet Bagel-style Black 40-inch Dog Bed	$ 110.98

In this second example, we know that the total sales amount of goods sold should be very close to the value of goods shipped. To see when these values are equal, look for where the lines overlap in the illustration.

2011 looks great, but what happened in 2010?
Remember to investigate why the 2010 lines are different
(the dark line is the left axis, and the light line is the right axis)

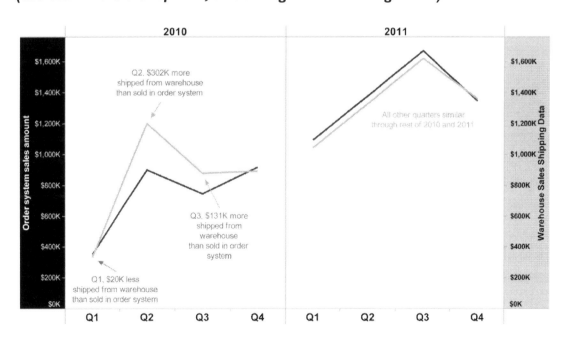

External checks: Look at the outside world

You may be able to look outside your company for confirmation of your results, especially if you are working with sales, marketing, financial or product development data. If it is available publicly, information about both competitors and complementary businesses may be useful. Here is a simple example: if revenue of your main competitor grew 10%, and your revenue also grew 10%, then your results appear to be reasonable.

Your results may be correct even if they are inconsistent, and you may even find out something interesting that you didn't know. Let's say both you and your competitor had revenue growth of 10%, but your customer base grew 2%, and your competitor's grew 10%. This may spell out trouble for your future, because you didn't acquire as many new customers as your competitor (although it is a possibility that your new customers are much bigger spenders).

BONUS TOOL. PROTECT YOUR ASSETS:
A LITTLE DATA MAINTENANCE GOES A LONG WAY

This section addresses the need for some "housekeeping" advice, such as naming files or folders clearly and consistently, making notes on your work and findings to date, and backing up and adding version numbers to your files if necessary. While very few people do this well, you can avoid a lot of frustration if you work at keeping up-to-date in this area.

When naming your files or folders, the more descriptive the name, the better. Using cryptic naming abbreviations can be confusing when you or someone else looks at it later. To keep track of updated versions, you can add the current date at the end of the file name. For example, for December 31, 2011, 2011_12_31 may be useful. Also, version numbers such as V1, V2, V3 may be a great alternative. Additionally, if it may be difficult to figure out what the data items are from their names, or if acronyms are used, maintain a list of definitions, and share it with others who may use the dataset.

Heads Up

If you rely on the automatic date label that your software adds whenever you open and change a file as a way to identify and find files, confusion may result.

You may have updated the file since you performed the analysis to correct a typo or make some minor changes. This forces the date to be updated when the bulk of the analysis was done earlier.

To remember the steps you've performed in collecting and cleaning up your data, you might choose to keep notes or a list directly in the spreadsheet file (using another worksheet in the overall spreadsheet), or in a separate text or spreadsheet file in the same folder. Include the data sources and how you combined the data for analysis (and clean-up details after you read *The Fourth C: Clean Up Your Data*).

Also, depending on where and how your data files are stored (your laptop, your PC at work, USB drives), make sure to back up any important files so you have a recovery file for valuable analyses.

Helpful Hint

Sharing data, reports, presentations, and analysis documents with your colleagues can be challenging for everyone involved.

When using a shared drive, organizing the files first by department, then by project or subject, is useful. However, while shared drives can work for small teams, they are less efficient for larger ones, since users need institutional knowledge to find files.

A product that we like, and that also has gotten positive reviews from clients, is SharePoint from Microsoft. SharePoint allows you to easily share your content and make it searchable, safe and available from any browser.

Taking the time to do all of this may be frustrating, but there are both immediate and long-term benefits. It may help you find errors. If you get lost in your own analysis, or come back to it after a long break, then you will save time and frustration. Also, other people will be able to figure out what you have done, which will save you the time and embarrassment of them having to track you down. Don't get discouraged—it may take a while to discover a method that works well for you.

FYI

Labeling and organizing your files well enough so that you and others can figure out later what you did is called **documentation**.

If you mention documentation to experienced analysts, you will invariably get a groan, because documenting work well is a never-ending challenge for everyone.

RECAP OF THE THIRD C: CHECK OUT YOUR DATA

In this C, you've begun to review your data and to obtain actionable insights to help you and others make better decisions about your business.

Data review toolkit

	TOOL	ACTION
1	**Sort**	Reorder your data
2	**Filter**	Focus on the right data
3	**Summary values**	Condense your data items for simplicity
	Sum	Add up your data values
	Count	How many do you have?
	Maximum and Minimum	The highs and lows of your data
	Span	The ranges of values in your data
	Average	Typical values for your data items
4	**Ranking**	Arrange data from top to bottom
	Median	Half are above, half are below
	Percentiles	Divide your data up into equal parts

	TOOL	ACTION
5	**Change over time**	Show how your data fluctuate or vary
6	**Reality checks**	Consider data in the context of your business
	Internal checks	Use company information as a benchmark
	External checks	Look at the outside world
Bonus	**Protect your assets**	A little data maintenance goes a long way

For your reference, keep notes or a list of what you've found during your data review.

Helpful Hint
If you collect a new dataset, don't forget to come back to this C to find out what's changed.

THE FOURTH C:
CLEAN UP YOUR DATA

Do what you can with what you have where you are.

—THEODORE ROOSEVELT
Cowboy, soldier, historian and
26th President of the U.S.

Data collected from the real world are messy! No company can claim they have perfect or complete data—most of you have probably experienced this firsthand. Employees or customers entering data into a computer can hit the wrong keys or forget to enter fields. Analysts mislabel units and make errors when doing calculations. Automatic data collectors (such as customer counters at store entrances or the automated coupon dispensers at the grocery store) may be on the fritz. Computers sometimes garble data because of software bugs or bad data coding rules (especially when converting one file format to another). Data formats become obsolete as software changes.

However, you can do a lot to clean up the mistakes and inaccuracies in your data. This is a necessary step, but it's often overlooked when people are in a rush. Note that we are not talking about cleaning up the entire company's main data sources or the data store (also called a "data warehouse" or a "data mart")—luckily for you, you probably will not be responsible for this task. We are instead referring to the data download or pull that you will be using in your analysis.

We've heard a story from a marketing analyst who was new to the company and was preparing an expensive catalog mailing to the customers in the top 10% (decile) of spending. Before he got there, the customers had been ranked from 1 to 10. He didn't verify the ranking scheme, and assumed that customers labeled "1" were the best ones. Unfortunately, these were actually the bottom decile of customers, who all received the mailing. The mailing definitely did not meet management expectations, but fortunately he kept his job.

We could fill an entire book with stories like these, but the point is it's well worth the modest investment of time to verify that the data you have are actually in the shape that you think they are in.

We've divided data clean-up into two sections. The first emphasizes **Do-It-Yourself Quick Fixes** that you can use to clean up errors that are relatively easy to find. The second reviews methods that apply to **data challenges which are company-based**, but that you should be aware of. You may even be able to do something about them.

Helpful Hint

The Fifth C: Chart Your Analysis and *The Sixth C: Customize Your Analysis* describe additional techniques that can help you find and correct many of these issues.

DO-IT-YOURSELF (DIY) QUICK FIXES, WHEN YOU HAVE DIRECT CONTROL OVER THE DATA

As technology advances,
it reverses the characteristics of every situation
again and again.
The age of automation is going to be
the age of "do it yourself".

—MARSHALL MCLUHAN (1957)
Media scholar who predicted the Internet decades beforehand

In this section, we'll explain the following five Quick Fixes. For your reference, we've compiled more detailed information about the Quick Fixes in a table in the Recap for this C.

Quick Data Fixes

#1.   Outliers

#2.   Missing data

- Records or rows
- Columns
- Data within scope

#3.   Date problems

- Wrong date window
- Relevant time period

#4.   Calculated field issues

- Errors in calculated fields
- "Hardcoding" calculated fields

#5.   Technical glitches

- Limitations of analysis software
- Confusion about data format

Quick Fix #1. Outliers

Looking for data points that are out of place and don't fit in with the rest of the data is a great way to catch a problem. An outlier may be an obvious mistake to be corrected, such as a product costing $1000 when the maximum price of an item in your inventory should be $100. Or it may be a correct value that you or someone else may be able to explain. For example, if your lowest-price item is $10, and you have a $5 minimum value in your data, it may be a special overstock item that was sold at a 50% discount. In addition to maximum and minimum, average and span may also help you find outliers.

The illustration shows the product lines that have outlying transaction amounts.

Are these data points accurate?
The outliers are pointed out in the graph

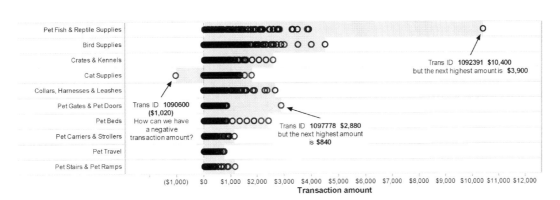

Helpful Hint

Your data review tools: what can't they do?

Not only can your data review tools from *The Third C: Check Out Your Data* help you see what you have, they can help you see what you should get rid of.

Just a reminder: we recommend keeping notes or a list of the changes that you've made to your data for your reference.

Heads Up

It is often valuable to keep your original dataset intact by making corrections to a second, duplicate copy with a different name.

This is useful if you make a mistake when deleting or fixing your data, and need to start over, or in case you need to refer to the original dataset.

Quick Fix #2. Missing data

Records or rows

Do you have all the records of interest? If you know you have more than **2,000** customers, and a count tells you that have only **1,000**, you are missing records. This is useful in case some of the data hasn't arrived into the source system yet or if your data pull was specified incorrectly.

Columns

Do you have all the data items or variables of interest? Review the columns that are in your dataset. You may have pulled sales data, when you actually need sales and returns data.

In the illustration, we counted our customers by month for 2011. This helped us find out that we were probably missing customers in December.

Look at the outlier in customer count
What happened to our customers in December?

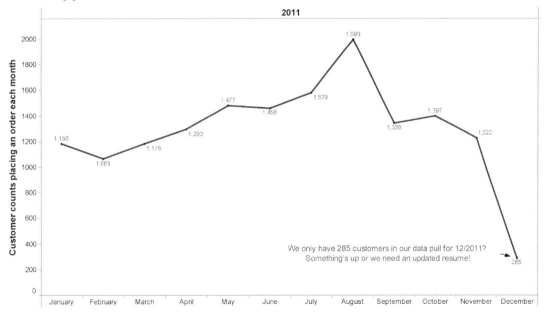

99

Data within scope

Double-check that you have the correct dataset for your question of interest. You may want data for your London stores, and realize that you chose Paris. You may have pulled an entire year's worth of data, but only needed the last quarter. You may have selected the entire customer database, but only wanted new customers.

In the illustration, management was interested in purple sparkle dog collars sold in 2011.

We pulled too much data

Product Name	2010	2011
Sparehand Auto Pet Safety Barrier/ Safety Guard		1
Sparkle Paw 11-inch Dog Collar and Lead Set-Purple	1	2
Sparkle Paw 14-inch Dog Collar and Lead Set-Purple		1
Sparkle Paw 18-inch Dog Collar and Lead Set-Purple	1	1
Sparkle Paw 18-inch Dog Collar-BlueBird	1	

This is what management wanted:
Purple sparkle dog collars sold in 2011

Product Name	2011
Sparkle Paw 11-inch Dog Collar and Lead Set-Purple	2
Sparkle Paw 14-inch Dog Collar and Lead Set-Purple	1
Sparkle Paw 18-inch Dog Collar and Lead Set-Purple	1

Quick Fix #3. Date problems

Wrong date window

Examine the date fields in your data pull to verify that the data are from the correct date window. We're interested in the Thanksgiving to Christmas time period for 2011, but the illustration shows that we pulled the 2010 data.

These aren't 2011 data!

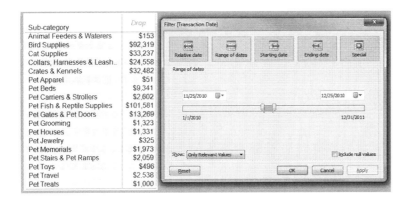

Relevant time period

Choosing the relevant time period usually requires understanding how your business works, so if you don't know, ask the person who would know about the details of a useful time frame. If reports about late sales or fixed transactions weren't entered into the database on time, key information that you assumed was there may be missing.

If you extracted the data for last year's sales on January 2nd, yet most returns from the holiday season weren't entered in until the end of January, you didn't include some very important data. In these illustrations we show the differences in returns once we included the whole month of January.

That's great—returns were only 4.8% of holiday sales
But wait, something's not right—
this only includes data through January 2

	Sold, not returned	% sold, not returned	Returned	% returned
Pet Fish & Reptile Supplies	$91,108	97.1%	$2,734	2.9%
Bird Supplies	$76,306	92.6%	$6,087	7.4%
Cat Supplies	$30,342	97.3%	$832	2.7%
Crates & Kennels	$28,937	94.7%	$1,631	5.3%
Collars, Harnesses & Leashes	$20,935	94.1%	$1,316	5.9%
Pet Gates & Pet Doors	$11,487	97.1%	$345	2.9%
Pet Beds	$8,784	97.0%	$271	3.0%
Pet Travel	$2,378	93.7%	$160	6.3%
Pet Stairs & Pet Ramps	$1,975	100.0%	$0	0.0%
Pet Carriers & Strollers	$2,262	88.2%	$304	11.8%
Pet Memorials	$1,686	93.8%	$111	6.2%
Grand Total	*$276,200*	*95.2%*	*$13,791*	*4.8%*

Returns are actually 11.8%
when we include all of January, the final return date

	Sold, not returned	% sold, not returned	Returned	% returned
Pet Fish & Reptile Supplies	$91,108	91.6%	$8,317	8.4%
Bird Supplies	$76,306	82.9%	$15,766	17.1%
Cat Supplies	$30,342	91.7%	$2,755	8.3%
Crates & Kennels	$28,937	89.4%	$3,435	10.6%
Collars, Harnesses & Leashes	$20,935	85.7%	$3,502	14.3%
Pet Gates & Pet Doors	$11,487	86.6%	$1,781	13.4%
Pet Beds	$8,784	94.0%	$556	6.0%
Pet Travel	$2,378	93.7%	$160	6.3%
Pet Stairs & Pet Ramps	$1,975	95.9%	$84	4.1%
Pet Carriers & Strollers	$2,262	88.2%	$304	11.8%
Pet Memorials	$1,686	85.5%	$287	14.5%
Grand Total	*$276,200*	*88.2%*	*$36,947*	*11.8%*

Quick Fix #4. Calculated field issues

Errors in calculated fields.

A calculated field is where you enter a formula in your analytical software to create a new data item. The formula can contain one or more data items as well as other values. For instance, if you would like to calculate amount of profit per salesperson, you may create a calculated field using the formula:

Profit per Salesperson = (Total Sales – Total Costs) / Number of Salespeople

Look for typos and outdated information in names or formulas. For instance, a field or item was moved or renamed from the last time you changed the formula, or your old formula for profit is no longer the correct formula.

Your product name may have changed. For example, you may have only had one product called "sparkle dog collar", but this year you are selling "gold sparkle dog collar" and "silver sparkle dog collar", so you need to update the names in your formulas.

Also, a common formula used by the company may have been changed. For instance, your old formula for profit didn't include losses from returns, but that is now included. When you change a key metric like profit, you could create another calculation showing the impact of the enhanced profit estimate formula versus the old profit formula, which is shown in the illustration.

Changing the calculated field for profit has a huge impact on certain product lines

	Transaction Amount	Estimated profit	Estimated profit returns included	Returns impact on profit
Bird Supplies	$92,072	$13,811	$9,613	-30.4%
Collars, Harnesses & Leashes	$24,438	$3,666	$2,720	-25.8%
Pet Memorials	$1,973	$543	$429	-20.9%
Pet Gates & Pet Doors	$13,269	$3,649	$2,945	-19.3%
Crates & Kennels	$32,372	$4,856	$3,929	-19.1%
Pet Carriers & Strollers	$2,566	$706	$586	-17.0%
Cat Supplies	$33,097	$4,965	$4,221	-15.0%
Pet Fish & Reptile Supplies	$99,425	$27,342	$24,230	-11.4%
Pet Travel	$2,538	$698	$635	-9.1%
Pet Beds	$9,341	$2,569	$2,349	-8.6%
Pet Stairs & Pet Ramps	$2,059	$566	$533	-5.9%

"Hardcoding" calculated fields

If you write a formula that is tied to your current business conditions or a specific set of data, known as **hardcoding** your formula, future datasets most likely won't show correct results.

For instance, a common issue is to hardcode the current year, such as entering in "2011" instead of referencing the Year data item, so that your fields won't work with next year's data. Another issue involves calculating values versus current targets or budgets. If you hardcode your budget or target at **$1,000,000**, this won't be correct if next year's budget or target changes. In the following illustration, the predicted sales (Budget sales) are shown for each quarter of 2010 and 2011. You can see there are likely two issues with the formula for budget sales: the values are identical for 2010 and 2011 (possible, but unlikely in most companies) and the formula will return the same result for budget sales by quarter forever.

Same amounts for budgeted sales for 2010 and 2011?
Evidence of a hardcoded value

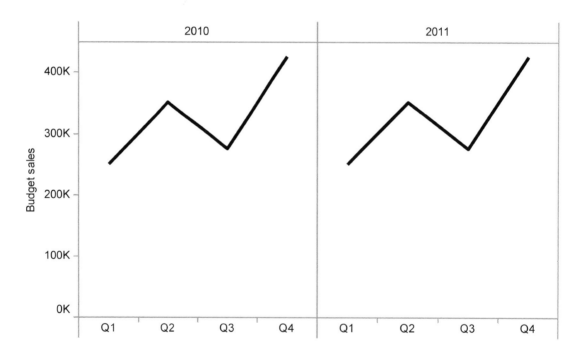

Quick Fix #5. Technical glitches

Limitations of analysis software

The most common example of a limitation of your software is when you try to download too many columns or records for your software to handle, and a portion of your data gets cut off. Often, you may not even get an error message. Check for missing rows or columns

Confusion about data format

Data items may be stored in an unexpected format. For example, sales amounts are in local currency, such as British pounds or Euros, while you think they're all saved in U.S. dollars. To correct this problem, examine data labels and look at formulas for calculated fields. Additionally, since many companies have databases that have been cobbled together over the years, perhaps even from mergers with other companies, you may encounter peculiarities, such as some of the online orders being stored in a separate system while others are in the traditional sales system.

Helpful Hint
After the DIY fixes, briefly check out the raw data.
Look at the first few records, and then choose a small random sample to see if it makes sense.

DATA CHALLENGES
THAT YOU MAY HAVE LIMITED CONTROL OVER
(BUT THAT YOU CAN STILL PATCH UP)

All things are difficult before they are easy.

—THOMAS FULLER
17th-century preacher and historian
and one of the first professional British writers

Data challenges over which you may have limited control are typically company-wide problems: point of collection errors and issues that arise when multiple people are working with the same database. Even worse, how the data are stored today might be very different from how they were stored in your systems last year.

Here's a list of the data challenges that we describe in this section. For your reference, we include a table with more details in the recap.

Challenges

#1.   Collection Point Issues

- Incomplete information
- Misspellings and other typos
- High error rates
- Long-term solutions

#2.   Company Red-Tape Issues

- Inconsistency
- Data limitations
- High volatility
- Security issues

Challenge #1. Collection Point Issues: Errors at point-of-entry into the database

P̲oint-of-entry errors result in inaccurate or incomplete data being entered into the database. It is often very difficult to catch and correct these errors since it is likely the information doesn't exist anywhere else. However, there are a few things that you can do.

Incomplete information

Check for empty fields by searching for null values.

In the following illustrations, something strange was going on with product price.

Why does Product Price have blank cells?

Looks like the data were incorrectly entered or imported into the next field

	A	I	J	K
1	Product SKU	Product Origin	Product Price	Long Description
46	10875125	CN		119.99
47	10875126	CN		49.49
48	10875127	CN		96.99 Give your cat a playground with this awesome Bungalow tree condo
49	10875128	CN		59.99

Misspellings and other typos

These can be accidental, such as entering the wrong zip code, or the result of a lack of standardized spellings of names, such as entering "New York City" when it should be abbreviated as NYC.

One way to catch these is with a count. For instance, your data contain sales by state, but you count 57 states. Another way to find these is to search for the duplicate records that can occur from misspellings and typos. For example, you may have two records with the same order ID, but order IDs are supposed to be unique; or the same customer has two records, such as Joe Perez in New York City and Joe Perez in NYC. To find these, use a pivot table and look for entries with a much smaller number of records, or adjacent entries with slightly different spellings.

The illustration shows duplicates as a result of misspellings and abbreviations.

Action item: standardize spellings

Manufacturer	Count
Aqua Vista	1
Aquavista	1
Hill & Dale	14
Hill And Dale	5
Majestic Pet Product	1
Majestic Pet Products	131
MPP	2
Precision	10
Precision Pet	87
Rough Rough & Meow	1
Ruff Ruff & Meow	60
Ruff Ruff and Meow	1

Helpful Hint

If you have many data items and do not have time to look at each one for duplicates, choose the ones that are the most important for your analysis.

High error rates

If you have a way to check the accuracy of your data (for instance, you have the data item of interest present in another dataset), you may want to estimate error rates. Do this by first taking a sample of your data and then checking every value in the sample. The number of incorrect values divided by the total number of values will tell you the rate of incorrect values (multiply by 100 to obtain a percentage).

For example, you have a dataset of recent sales transactions. You would like to check the error rate for customer address, and you have access to the separate customer database kept up-to-date by your company. If you look at 100 transactions, and five of them have the wrong customer address as compared to the customer database, your error rate is 5/100 = 0.05, or 5%, and 95% of your data are correct.

Heads Up
In larger companies, it is nearly impossible to have a dataset with no errors. In general, the lowest percentage of bad data that you will likely attain is **1-3%**. In reality, a lot of data that has never been verified may be **10-30% incorrect**, based on counting errors in one or more of the fields. Certain fields that are critical to your analysis may require a much lower error rate, so focus on getting these cleaned up instead of trying to clean up the entire dataset.

Long-term solutions

While there is no means to prevent all point-of-entry errors from occurring, there are some ways to help. Urge management to establish and circulate rules for employees that describe standardized point-of-entry procedures. Have the database experts restrict what can be entered into fields so that employees will be prompted when common mistakes occur, before their entry is accepted.

For instance, if a required field is not filled out, or if four numbers are entered in for a U.S. zip code instead of five, the employees would not be allowed to continue in their data entry. Unfortunately, the programs behind these systems can often contain hidden mistakes too. Work closely with your IT team to verify data entry rules and recalibrate automated data collectors often.

Challenge #2. Company Red-Tape Issues: Resulting from different people and departments working on the same database

Inconsistency

This is one of the biggest problems that occurs when multiple people are working on the same project.

Different people or business units using

- different codes for the same thing
- the same codes for different things
- different formulas for a data item, but calling it the same name (such as *Sales* referring to either gross sales or net sales)
- the same formula, but calling it different names
- different formatting rules

Helpful Hint

Keep an eye out for repeating error types that can be fixed automatically.

For example, if the product code has been changed, automatically change the old code to the new one, as the old code enters the source database.

Heads Up

If you repeatedly see an unusual value for a data item, such as *999* or *-1* or *999999999*, it probably has a special meaning that is worth investigating.

Long-term solutions involve coordination

- create a data dictionary to circulate to colleagues, by compiling:
  - standardized codes or formatting rules
  - how the company calculates data items in different departments
- to identify problem areas, consider starting or participating in a periodic, scheduled data quality review with various departments
- obtain the support of upper management to prioritize high-quality data

We admit that these solutions are usually as difficult to accomplish as they appear, but in the least, keep up-to-date on the data items most important to you.

Heads Up

Joining datasets (covered earlier in *The Second C: Collect Your Data*) will be difficult and likely result in missing rows if there are inconsistent names of key data items.

Helpful Hint

People who are responsible for particular datasets commonly complain that colleagues who have access often change data, labels, formats, etc., without permission.

For workplace harmony, it's a good idea to check with the owner before altering a dataset.

Data limitations

At some point, everyone is frustrated by the limitations of the available data. If it is important enough, try to research these issues. You may be able to find the cause of the problem and hopefully a solution.

Common limitations include out-of-date data, in which the data are too old to answer your questions, and missing information, in which crucial details about the dataset or essential data items were never documented or are unavailable.

High volatility

If you frequently find inaccurate or missing values in different places at different times, and there seems to be no pattern or explanation, your data could be considered highly volatile. This often occurs when many people in a company use the database (the more people or the more departments, the worse the problem), but no one person or group has ownership of it. Alternatively, there may be people responsible for the database, but they are overwhelmed with the amount of work it takes to manage it, or it may not be a priority for this team. High volatility may also be a problem if you use a system that works with many other systems, since bad data may be allowed to sneak in through these other systems.

High volatility requires a very intensive, long-term, company-wide solution to fix. What can you do in the meantime? Be vigilant in checking data when updating critical reports or analyses, because the data may have changed from the last time.

Security issues

These will come into play when you think that there may be a problem with the data, but you are not able to access the details due to security restrictions. Try to track down the people who can possibly give you access. If you're not allowed, you may have to give them your summarized results so they can perform critical checks with the detailed, secured data. Security issues are a big problem for larger corporations and financial-service companies.

Heads Up

If you collect new data later in the analysis, it is crucial that you return to this C to find and correct mistakes and problems.

RECAP OF THE FOURTH C: CLEAN UP YOUR DATA

*Errors using inadequate data are much less
than those using no data at all.*

—CHARLES BABBAGE
"father of the programmable computer"

- Data collected from the real world are messy.

- However, you can do a lot to clean up the mistakes and inaccuracies in your data.

- We describe how to clean up two different types of data issues, which are summarized in tables on the following pages:

    — Do-It-Yourself (DIY) Quick Fixes that you can use to clean up errors that are relatively easy to find

    — Methods that apply to data challenges that are company-wide

DIY Quick Data Fixes

DIY QUICK FIX	LOOKING FOR CLUES
Outliers	
	Use max, min, average, and span to find
Missing data	
Records or rows	Count number of rows or transactions
Columns	Count number of columns or data items
Data within scope	Match dataset to question of interest
Date problems	
Wrong date window	Check date window against question of interest
Relevant time period	Compare time period to business-specific details
Calculated field issues	
Errors in calculated fields	Typos and outdated information in names and formulas
"Hardcoding" calculated fields	Formulas with a specific number value that will never change, even as the data update
Technical glitches	
Limitations of analysis software	Verify that the download doesn't have more data than the application can read and that the
Confusion about data format	Look closely at labels and units

Data Challenges that you may have limited control over

DATA CHALLENGE	LOOKING FOR CLUES
Collection Point Issues	
Incomplete information	Find empty fields by searching for null values
Misspellings and other typos	Use frequency counts and look for duplicate records
High error rates	Select a sample of your data to estimate error rates
Long-term solutions	Create list of rules for colleagues, restrict what can be entered in data fields, check computer automation
Company Red-Tape Issues	
Inconsistency	Verify that different people or business units are using the same codes, formulas, and names by circulating lists or hosting regular data reviews with key departments
Data limitations	Look for out-of-date and missing information
High volatility	Repeated inaccurate or missing values in different places at different times
Security issues	Can't access data but not sure why

Now that you have collected, checked out, and cleaned up your data, you've done all that you can to ensure that your data are ready for the next challenge—the analysis. So move on to *Analysis In Action: Introduction to the Fifth and Sixth C's.*

Visit **http://www.AccidentalAnalyst.com** *to sign up for our newsletter with information about upcoming live training, webinars, tips, books and more!*

ANALYSIS IN ACTION: THE FIFTH AND SIXTH C'S

Do the simplest thing that could possibly work.

—WARD CUNNINGHAM
Computer programmer and inventor of the first wiki

Now that you've won the battle to whip your data into shape, you are ready to win the war by moving on to the analysis. Many accidental analysts get stuck here trying to figure out what to do next! The most common first step is to do some detective work by trying to figure out what other people have done in the past (which hopefully will give you some helpful hints). Or you may attempt to translate the report your boss wants into an analysis. In recent years, you may have started searching the internet for relevant information. If you are really lucky, you have an expert you can work closely with to learn through practical experience.

If you have a lot of time to figure things out, or access to a local expert, these are all reasonable ways to get started on your analysis.

However, the typical challenge facing an accidental analyst is to arrive at solutions to business problems within a short period of time, so the solutions are still relevant to the situation (and to your boss). You probably won't want to start a complex analysis—all you need are clear yet valuable tools and techniques to quickly assess the problem and take action. The next two C's contain a do-it-yourself guide of analysis techniques that you can use to answer everyday business questions for you, your colleagues, and your clients.

These techniques are demonstrated by general business questions that use data items such as sales and profit, which are familiar to people in any line of work. You may have the same questions, but most likely you will need to adjust the techniques to fit your particular problem, depending upon your business, department, and role. So, these techniques are intended as examples to help you both frame and answer your questions. Also, since a vast majority of business situations can be investigated with just these fundamental approaches, we are intentionally excluding complex analysis techniques that you may have heard of, such as modeling or forecasting. While advanced techniques can be invaluable, there are already many books that focus on them.

THE FIFTH C: CHART YOUR ANALYSIS

In this C, we demonstrate practical solutions to common problems that we call **business scenarios**. You'll learn how to analyze the scenarios applying **visual analytics**, which is simply organizing your data in the most useful chart, whether table or graph, to answer questions. We also include a multitude of examples and expert tips and tricks.

THE SIXTH C: CUSTOMIZE YOUR ANALYSIS

Using a realistic, case study approach, we build upon the information from the previous C's, so that you'll be able to customize or "fine-tune" your analysis to fit specific questions. This C follows an analyst during a highly interactive series of meetings with the sales department while she answers most of their questions on the spot, giving you a sense of what you may experience in a similar meeting with colleagues.

Heads Up
Verify that you haven't already answered some of your questions in the earlier data check-up or clean-up C's.
Why do additional analysis if you don't need to? You might even save enough time to finish ahead of schedule.

THE FIFTH C:
CHART YOUR ANALYSIS

An approximate answer to the right problem
is worth a good deal more
than an exact answer to an approximate problem.

—JOHN TUKEY
Prominent American statistician
who first used the word "software"

The goal of analysis is to answer questions. Many common business questions can be answered by displaying or **charting** the data in an appropriate table or graph. This C describes ten scenarios based on these questions, listed at the end of this introduction. Each scenario focuses on the goal that you are trying to accomplish with your analysis, such as comparing different categories or determining if you reached a goal.

With a brief description and a thumbnail sketch, we introduce you to the chart type or types that you can use to reach these goals. Using data from a pet supply company, we then demonstrate a specific example of the scenario and how to analyze it. The point is to provide ideas about how you could tackle similar problems. For your reference, we also include additional details about each chart type, along with *Expert tips* on the best ways to use the chart and *Pitfalls* where people often take a wrong turn with it.

Helpful Hint

When you are choosing which chart type to use for the question at hand, keep yourself on track by asking:
- "What question am I trying to answer?"
- "Does this chart answer it?"

There are several specialized chart types that we don't cover in detail, but they may help you in the future. We have included summaries and introductory examples in *FYI boxes*—make sure to research the details before you use them.

This C is intended to help you to think about your problem from an analytic mindset. While we cover some basic scenarios and examples, your particular problems most likely will be different, since there are endless possibilities, depending upon the type of business. Additionally, if you follow our approach and frame your questions in simple terms referring to the problem that you are trying to solve, you'll be able to describe your analysis to colleagues in terms they can understand.

FYI

You may have heard of the term **data visualization** that is often used when discussing data analysis.

Though it sounds technical, this simply means displaying your data effectively so that you or others can easily understand what's going on. In other words, are your graphs and tables getting your message across to help people understand the problem and make a decision? This C focuses on using good data visualization techniques by organizing your data with the *appropriate* chart, whether table or graph, to answer previously identified questions, which is the practice of **visual analytics**.

A related term is "**viz**", which refers to a table or graph.

BEST-CASE BUSINESS SCENARIOS:
USER-FRIENDLY SOLUTIONS
TO COMMON BUSINESS PROBLEMS

#1.   When precision matters: *Compare exact values*

#2.   Winners and losers: *Compare different categories at a glance*

#3.   Extreme comparisons: *Go beyond basic bar charts to compare between and within categories*

#4.   Time travel: *Examine how your data change over time*

#5.   Was it worth the cost? *Determine Return on Investment (ROI)*

#6.   Did I measure up? *Reach your goal*

#7.   Little things add up: *Graph cumulative results*

#8.   Where the action is: *Map your data*

#9.   The story is in the details: *Expand the details of important data items*

Bonus. Frequency of occurrences

Bonus. Relationships

#10.   Try, try again: *Revisit the question if you didn't get it right the first time*

SCENARIO #1. WHEN PRECISION MATTERS: COMPARE EXACT VALUES

In this scenario, we describe *tables* and *highlight tables* in detail, for when you need exact numbers to answer your business questions. We also introduce *heat maps*, a special type of table.

Tables

If you need to compare exact values with each other, start with a *table*. Businesspeople are usually very familiar with tables because they are in a spreadsheet format, like Excel.

First, here is a thumbnail sketch so you have a general idea of what we're talking about (don't worry about the details yet).

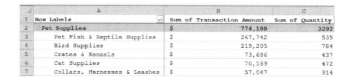

Row Labels	Sum of Transaction Amount	Sum of Quantity
Pet Supplies	$ 774,188	3292
Pet Fish & Reptile Supplies	$ 267,742	535
Bird Supplies	$ 219,205	784
Crates & Kennels	$ 73,686	437
Cat Supplies	$ 70,189	472
Collars, Harnesses & Leashes	$ 57,047	314

We'll start with an example of how to answer a business question using a table. The shipping department is counting their inventory, and some of their *Leopard-print Dog Beds* are missing. The number of dog beds sold should be equal to the number of dog beds shipped. You must find any counts that are different, which you can do by comparing the exact counts.

Detailed tables are great when looking for exact values

Transaction ID	Sold	Shipped	Difference
4787226	1	3	2
1177702	1	3	2
1203149	3	4	1
731107	2	3	1
4341089	1	2	1
4362680	1	2	1
4077840	1	2	1
2016294	1	2	1
96779	1	2	1
2632718	1	2	1
4089470	1	2	1
437958	1	2	1
1671579	9	9	0
4408770	9	9	0
4085122	9	9	0
1438739	9	9	0

You accidently shipped more dog beds than you sold! Note that the relevant cells are highlighted in gray for easy reference.

Another example of where tables are useful is in human resources. There's a salesperson who has problems organizing receipts from business trips. You want to compare his submitted spreadsheet of travel expenses with corporate credit card statements and travel policy, and find the ones that are different.

These last two examples demonstrate the simplest kind of table, which displays all the data values, also commonly called a listing or report. However, people often use tables that contain only summary values, such as sum and average (covered in detail in *The Third C: Check Out Your Data*). These are called *summary tables*, *cross-tabs*, or *pivot tables*.

In the last illustration, you noticed that you shipped more dog beds than you sold. Now you're wondering if that has happened with other products. You create a summary table with the product lines. You include the sum of the quantity sold and the sum of the quantity shipped.

Summary table to compare *sums* of items sold versus shipped

	A	B	C
	Row Labels	Sum of Quantity sold	Sum of Quantity shipped
	⊞ Bird Supplies	784	811
	⊞ Cat Supplies	478	488
	⊞ Collars, Harnesses & Leashes	316	320
	⊞ Pet Apparel	7	10
	⊞ Pet Beds	236	239
	⊞ Pet Fish & Reptile Supplies	547	569
	⊞ Pet Houses	24	24
	⊞ Pet Jewelry	19	20
	⊞ Pet Toys	8	8
	⊞ Pet Travel	65	64
	Grand Total	2484	2553

There definitely is a problem here—for most of the product lines, you shipped more than you sold (and for *Pet Travel*, you sold more than you shipped, which is a whole other problem).

Depending on your department and problem at hand, summary tables are typically more useful for analysis than just a listing of all the values, since they offer an overview of what's going on rather than overloading you with every detail of what happened.

It's helpful to become familiar with table terminology, which we first describe and then display in the next illustration. Each individual box in the table is called a *cell*. A vertical stack of cells is called a *column*. Each column typically contains a single *data item*, which is also referred to as a *data field*, a *measure*, a *metric*, or a *variable*. The first cell of each column typically contains the name of the data item, technically called a *header* or *label*.

A horizontal line of cells stretching across the table is a *row*. Rows typically contain individual *records, observations,* or *transactions.*

What's in a spreadsheet?

	A	B	C	D	E	F	G	H	I	J	K	L
1		Column	OR	Data Item	OR	Data Field	OR	Measure	OR	Metric	OR	Variable
2	**Row**	cell										
3	OR			cell								
4	**Record**					cell						
5	OR							cell				
6	Observation									cell		
7	OR											cell
8	**Transaction**											

Heads Up

It is not unusual to see spreadsheets that are reversed. The individual records might be in the columns and the data items or metrics might be in the rows.

Your analysis will be easier if you "swap" or "pivot" the rows and columns, so that records are in rows and metrics are in columns, because you usually will have a lot more records than metrics. This will make sense as you gain more experience, but here's an example of one of the issues.

You have a few metrics for the years 2010, 2011, and 2012, and it seems like it doesn't matter which are placed in rows versus columns. However, now you need to look at those metrics for every hour during each of the three years, which is a total of approximately 26,000 hours. In Excel 2010, you are limited to about 16,000 columns, but are allowed over 1,000,000 rows, so you only would be able to fit 26,000 hours in rows.

Most analytical tools, like Excel or Tableau Software, have a swap, pivot, or transpose feature.

Expert tips

- Use simple, powerful and relevant data items or metrics whenever possible so that the values are very clear and compelling. For instance, key metrics for the Sales Department might be *total sales (year-to-date)*, *target sales (year-to-date)*, and *percent achievement*.

- For easy reading and reference, shade alternate rows or columns, or groups of rows or columns.

Pitfalls

- Avoid tables if you don't require exact values or detailed precision—they can be difficult and time-consuming to read and interpret.

- Use only the metrics you need—too many will clutter the table.

Highlight tables

If you would like to emphasize particular values in your table so that they are easy to find, turn the text table into a *highlight table* by shading or coloring the cells to quickly identify and examine the important values.

For instance, you'd like to find the months and product lines that had the highest profits in 2011. To be able to quickly find them, you highlight the profits: the higher the profit, the darker the shading.

Highlight tables help you quickly find extreme values in your data

	2011											
	Q1			Q2			Q3			Q4		
	Jan	Feb	Mar	Apr	May	Jun	Jul	Aug	Sep	Oct	Nov	Dec
Crates & Kennels	$5,582	$5,378	$5,118	$6,371	$7,177	$7,396	$6,182	$10,745	$7,566	$7,704	$6,651	$6,879
Pet Gates & Pet Doors	$5,254	$5,011	$4,794	$6,822	$6,287	$6,476	$5,421	$7,834	$5,855	$5,198	$4,072	$5,040
Cat Supplies	$5,136	$4,538	$4,606	$4,513	$5,632	$5,178	$5,967	$6,721	$4,267	$4,271	$4,498	$5,026
Collars, Harnesses & Leashes	$4,272	$4,199	$3,177	$3,993	$5,178	$4,981	$5,980	$6,624	$4,543	$5,614	$4,276	$5,240
Pet Beds	$2,717	$3,352	$4,088	$4,244	$4,938	$4,722	$3,878	$7,013	$3,083	$2,986	$3,656	$4,095
Pet Carriers & Strollers	$1,115	$1,356	$1,182	$861	$929	$1,165	$1,597	$1,074	$877	$1,030	$887	$699
Pet Health		$10			$28	$6						
Pet Luxury			$10								$10	

The darker cells help you find the high profits, which occurred mostly in August for the five product lines at the top of the list. You can also quickly find the months and product lines that had no profit, which are the white cells.

Helpful Hint

Since this book is in black and white, we are much more limited than you typically will be in your work, unless you have to print something without color ink.

Expert tips

- It is typically most useful to use a continuum of colors to represent the range of values of a data item. For instance, color the values bright green to light green and light red to bright red, with green representing the "good" values, such as high profits, and red the "bad", such as low profits.

- If you are highlighting transactions with errors so that you remember to investigate them, color the cells red when they don't match, and green when they're okay—the further off the correct value, the brighter red the color.

- Keep in mind that about 5% of Americans are color blind, so if there's a good chance you may be showing your chart to one of them, use shading or a color-blind palette instead.

Pitfalls

- Don't confuse yourself or others by using too many colors.

- To make it easier to see the numbers, avoid using dark colors (unless you use white text) or coloring the text instead of the cells.

FYI

You can use *heat maps* if you would like the information in a table format, but don't need the exact values.

They're called heat maps because they indicate the "temperature" or intensity of a measure, making it quick and easy to spot extreme values: the *higher* the profit, the *darker* and *larger* the square.

They can fit in a smaller space than highlight tables.

A heat map is similar to a highlight table,
but the numbers are removed for faster examination

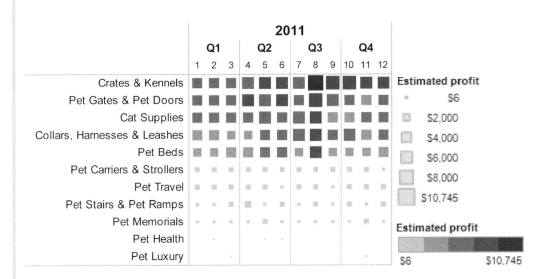

You can quickly come to the same conclusion that you had with the highlight table: you had high profits in August for certain product lines.

SCENARIO #2. WINNERS AND LOSERS
COMPARE DIFFERENT CATEGORIES AT A GLANCE

In this scenario, we cover *basic bar charts*, *multi-pane bar charts*, and *pie charts*, which are different options for quick comparison of multiple categories.

Basic bar charts

If you would like to quickly compare a single metric or data item across multiple categories, use a *bar chart* or *bar graph*. The value of the metric is represented by the height or length of the bar.

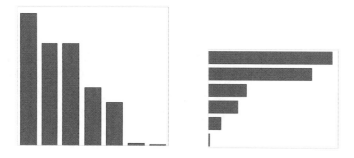

We'll start with a basic bar chart. Which product lines have the highest profit? You graph estimated profit by product line. The default order is alphabetical by product line.

**It's easy to pick out the high-profit product line,
but it can be easier...**

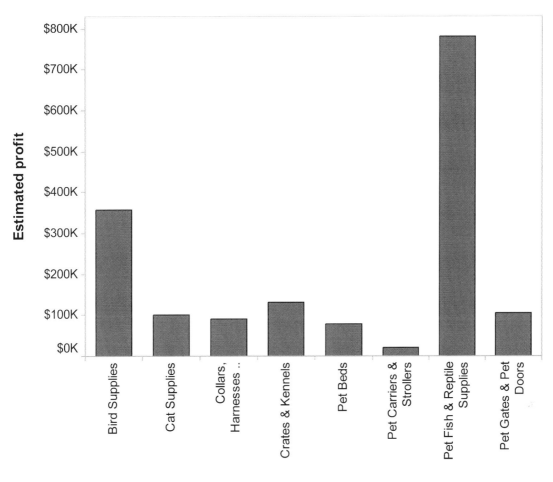

Although you quickly can pick out the high-profit product line, *Pet Fish & Reptile Supplies*, it is not so easy to pick out the fourth-highest profit product line, for example. Also, the names could be easier to read. So graph defaults are fine to start with, but they can hide key information.

Helpful Hint
If you flip the bars to be horizontal, they are usually easier to compare.
For this reason, we mostly use horizontal bar charts, if possible.

After *swapping* or *pivoting* the axes and sorting by profit

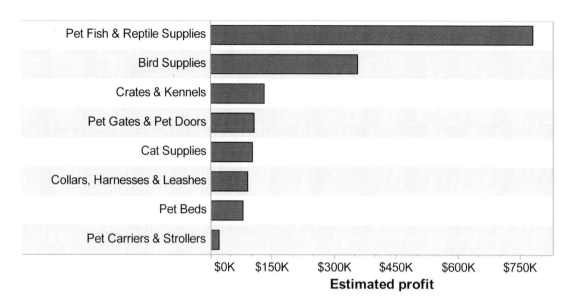

Notice how much easier it is to answer questions versus the last graph.

Basic bar charts are great for showing a single metric, such as profit, for multiple categories, such as product line. In general, bar charts are extremely flexible and allow you to easily see the overall trends in your data. They are useful for many questions that do not require the detailed information found in a text table.

Expert tips

- Bar charts are a simple and clear way to get your point across, so they are useful for reports or presentations.

- Sort according to the metric of interest.

Pitfalls

- Always include the zero-axis (start at the zero value) for any type of bar chart. If you don't, the graph will not accurately depict the data, because it will make the differences between the bars look larger than they are, as shown in the illustrations below.

Misleading without the zero-axis, since it looks like pet beds are just a few % of the top selling product line

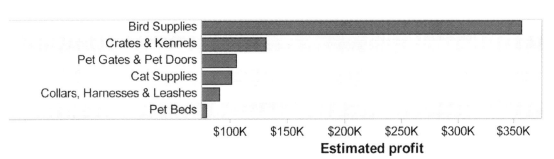

In reality, pet beds are about 20% of the amount of the top product line

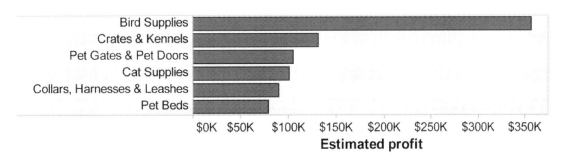

137

Multi-pane bar charts

Instead of one metric shown across multiple categories, as shown in the basic bar chart, you might want to compare several metrics across those categories, using *multi-pane bar charts*.

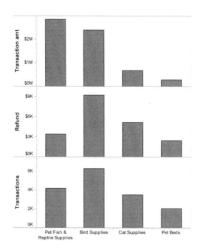

A multi-pane bar chart is essentially one large chart composed of more than one basic bar chart. A *pane* in a multi-pane bar chart is similar to a pane in a multi-pane window (in the thumbnail, there are three panes, each with four bars in it).

A sales manager asks to see three metrics to find out which product lines are driving sales. For the top six product lines, he wants total sales transaction amount and number of transactions. He also needs the average product price, to find out which product lines have the higher-priced products. You create three basic bar charts, one for each metric. You position them one on top of another—*aligned* by the product line categories for quick comparison (these charts are sometimes called *aligned bar charts* for this reason).

Three metrics in one chart—great for quick comparisons
The top product line isn't the same for all three

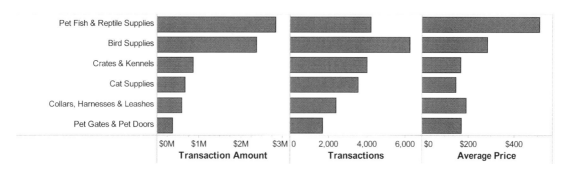

All three metrics are highest in *Pet Fish & Reptile Supplies* and *Bird Supplies*, and in general, the lowest in *Pet Gates & Pet Doors*.

Note that:

• Each pane can have metrics with different scales or units. They are still useful to compare because you can get a sense of the overall shape or trend.

• You can sort by only one of the metrics, or panes, at a time. The product lines are sorted in descending order by transaction amount.

Multi-pane bar charts can get quite complex, because you are able to add a second category for more detailed comparison. The sales manager now wants to see how these metrics look in the East versus the West. So, *product line* is the **primary category**, and region is the **secondary category**.

For more detail: the primary category, product line, is divided into a secondary category, region

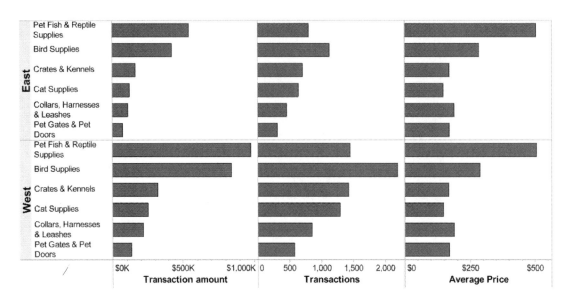

This is interesting. The West has higher transaction amounts and number of transactions than the East. However, average prices of the products sold in each product line is almost identical between the East and the West.

Heads Up

This graph takes up a lot of space, and North and South aren't even on it.

We address this problem using *stacked bar charts* in *Scenario #3, Extreme Comparisons*.

Now, we're going to take multi-pane bar charts to the next level. Consider showing *relative values* instead of *actual values* since they can make comparison across panes much easier.

The sales manager would like to quickly compare product lines between the North and the South. You decide to use relative values, specifically percentage of sales within each region.

By using relative values, such as % of region, you can quickly compare product lines across regions

Beyond the relative values, this is a little different than the other multi-pane bar charts, because each pane has the same metric, but for each of the two regions. The bars within each pane add up to 100%.

The *Pet Memorials* product line is the highest percentage of sales in the North, while *Pet Carriers & Strollers* represents the highest percentage of sales in the South. *Pet Apparel* doesn't do well in either region.

In summary, multi-pane bar charts are extremely flexible while remaining easy to discuss and understand.

Expert tips

- Sort by the primary metric of interest.

- If you have many bars in each pane, consider showing just the top 10 or 20 items by grouping the remaining items into an "Other" category.

- If you need a more compact view, try a *stacked bar chart*, shown later in this C.

Pitfalls

- Clearly labels the axes with the metric and units that you are using for that pane.

- Resist the temptation to use different colors or shading for each bar unless the colors mean something important. Your audience will be distracted by the colors when they have no particular meaning, directing them away from the overall shape of the data.

Pie charts

Perhaps you would like to quickly compare a few categories to gain a rough sense of which categories are larger and smaller relative to the combined total for all categories, often called "percentage of the whole" or relative contribution. If the exact numbers are not important, *pie charts* are a commonly used alternative.

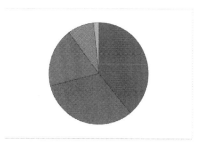

Heads Up

Experts overwhelmingly agree that it is extremely difficult to distinguish the sizes of the slices in pie charts, and advise against using them. Later in this section, we show an extreme example of a pie chart with too many slices.

However, they are easy to understand and have been used widely in business for a long time, so they are still a popular graph type in spite of their limitations. Whenever possible, we use bar charts instead of pie charts.

Your boss asks you for a pie chart of the top six product lines in average transaction amount, to show how important they are relative to each other.

Pie charts are useful only for simple comparisons

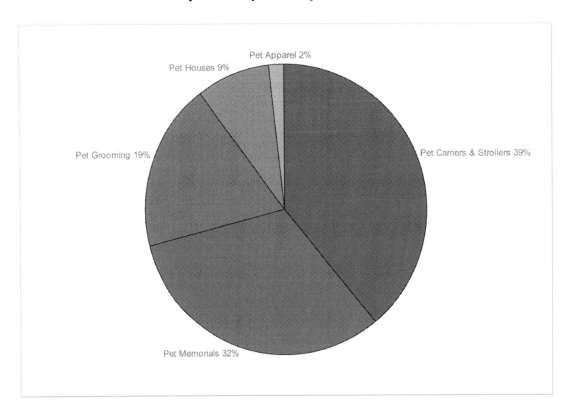

A quick glance can tell you that *Pet Carriers & Strollers* and *Pet Memorials* are almost tied for first place (note that you have to look at the labels to really be able to tell that *Pet Carriers & Strollers* is 7% higher).

You've known the way a pie chart works since you were a child trying to figure out which slice of pizza or cake was the largest. Pie charts show a snapshot in time and the key categories of data contributing to a particular situation, such as "Percentage of sales by salesperson" or "Pet beds sold by region".

Expert tips

- Use bar charts instead whenever possible, because it is easier to compare the categories, especially if the values are similar. *Stacked bar charts* are much easier to read (these are explained in *Scenario #3, Extreme comparisons,* below).

FYI

We're not trying to beat up on the pie chart users out there; we've used pie charts in the past before we learned about their disadvantages.

- Show percentages of the whole on the labels instead of values, such as "52% of the market" rather than "$36,000" (out of a total amount in the pie of $69,230) so people aren't forced to perform these calculations in their heads.

Heads Up

The percentages must add up to 100%.

We often see pie charts that are less than 100%. For instance, "Women that buy pet jewelry: 83%" and "Men that buy pet jewelry: 7%". The reader can assume that the data are missing on whether the other 10% are women or men, but avoid forcing your audience to do the calculations in their heads by putting in an "Unknown: 10%" slice.

We also see pie charts that add up to more than 100%—that detective work is a lot more difficult. If it's a slight amount over, it may be a rounding issue, in which decimals are rounded up to the next whole number, such as 95.5 turning into 96.

Both of these problems show up quite a bit in the popular media.

- If you choose to use pie charts, sort the slices in descending order by percentage amount or value, clockwise. This immediately shows the top to bottom categories.

- Similarly, shade or color the slices from dark to light in descending order.

Pitfalls

- If you have more than **6-8** categories, combine smaller categories into an "Other" slice or use a bar chart.

Don't cut your pie into more than seven or eight slices!
It's difficult to read the names and see differences by slice

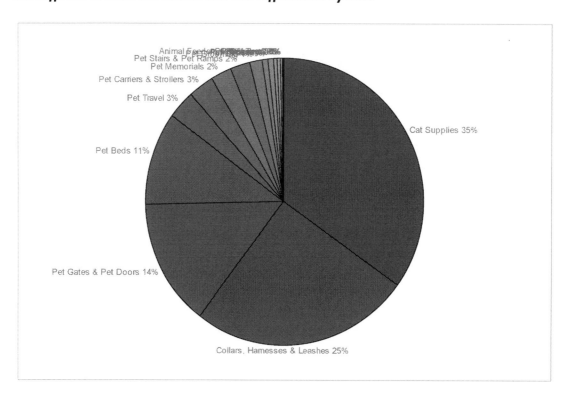

The product lines are easier to see in a bar chart

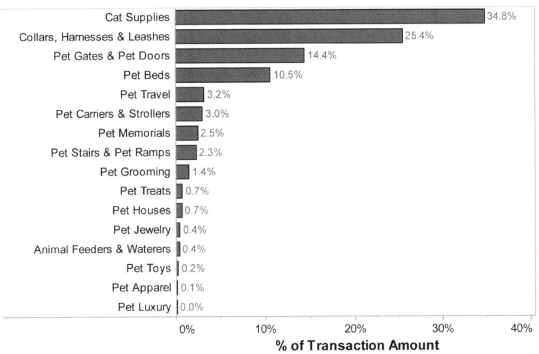

% of Transaction Amount

- Cat Supplies — 34.8%
- Collars, Harnesses & Leashes — 25.4%
- Pet Gates & Pet Doors — 14.4%
- Pet Beds — 10.5%
- Pet Travel — 3.2%
- Pet Carriers & Strollers — 3.0%
- Pet Memorials — 2.5%
- Pet Stairs & Pet Ramps — 2.3%
- Pet Grooming — 1.4%
- Pet Treats — 0.7%
- Pet Houses — 0.7%
- Pet Jewelry — 0.4%
- Animal Feeders & Waterers — 0.4%
- Pet Toys — 0.2%
- Pet Apparel — 0.1%
- Pet Luxury — 0.0%

- Even though your software allows it, don't use pie charts with negative values; how can you have a negative slice of pie (unless someone stole it)? Use bar charts instead

- Pie charts are not the best option for changes over time—use line charts instead (look at *Scenario #4, Time travel*).

- Using multiple pies, in which people have to compare and calculate amounts from pie-to-pie, is extremely confusing. You may remember questions like these from standardized tests in school. They weren't fun then, and they're not any better now!

Helpful Hint

We often have students ask how to convince their bosses, colleagues, or customers to stop asking for pie charts.

We suggest a gentle approach: give them the pie chart and then show them a bar chart. It might take a few tries, but hopefully they will see the advantages of the bar chart, especially if you point them out.

SCENARIO #3. EXTREME COMPARISONS: GO BEYOND BASIC BAR CHARTS TO COMPARE BETWEEN AND WITHIN CATEGORIES

In addition to allowing you to compare different categories, which you already can do with basic and multi-pane bar charts, this scenario gives you the power to make comparisons within the same categories.

So you can ask more complex questions, we'll show you how to include a lot more information in a bar chart with *stacked bar charts* and *bar charts with related metric displayed in shading (or color)*. We also explain *circle plots*, which share some similarities with bar charts, but which replace the bars with small circles.

Stacked bar charts

If you would like to compare actual values between primary categories, as well as actual values of the secondary categories within each primary category, use a stacked bar chart.

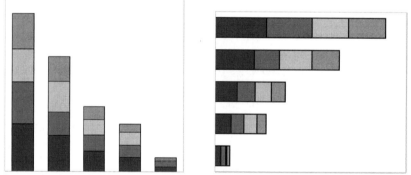

In one of the multi-pane bar chart illustrations, we were unable to fit a separate pane for each of the four regions on the page, so we included only the East and West. For easier comparison, it would be useful to have all four regions (East, West, North, and South) on one graph.

Stacked bar charts can do this. For example, you are interested in sales of the top five product lines for each region. To do this, you "stack" sales of each region on top of the product lines.

Stacked bar charts are a compact way to compare both the primary category (product line) and secondary category (region)

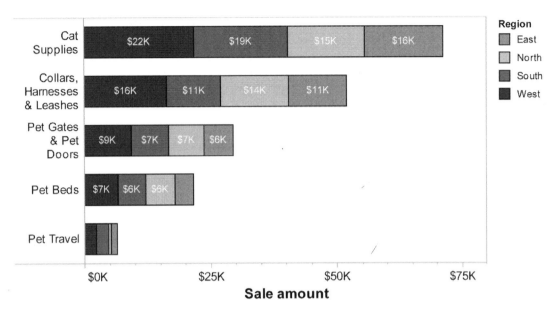

The five large bars are the primary category, the product lines, such as *Cat Supplies*. If you ignore the stacks, and only pay attention to the ends of the product line bars, this is similar to a basic bar chart, in which you can quickly review the overall trend across the primary category.

With the addition of the stacks within each bar, you can also study trends for sales of product lines within the secondary category, the region, which is defined in the legend. This is because the large bars are built of four smaller bars that represent the actual dollar sale amounts of each of the four regions for that product line.

For more clarity, the primary category is sorted by total sale amount for all four regions combined. *Cat Supplies* is the bestselling product line, *Collars, Harnesses & Leashes* is the second best, and so on. Also, by looking at the stacks, you can see that for almost all product lines, the West dominates sales, while the East is generally the lowest in sales.

Stacked bar charts can also be used to graph relative contribution by secondary category, so they are a good alternative to pie charts. For example, what if you want to figure out the relative contribution of each region to the total sales for that product line? Or, put another way, what percentage of the total sales for a specific product line are from the North, South, East and West?

By changing the labels to percentages, it is easy to compare relative contribution

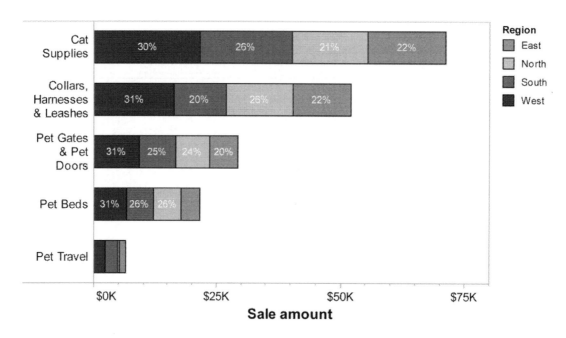

All four of these percentages, within each bar, should add up to 100%. This makes it much easier to compare the stacks. For instance, you can tell what percentage of sales in *Pet Gates & Pet Doors* occurs in the North.

If you are not as concerned with actual dollar amounts as you are with relative values, change the metric to percentage of total order amount to make the height of all five large bars 100%.

**Go one step further with percentages—
now you can easily read the percentages
for the smallest stacks from the last chart**

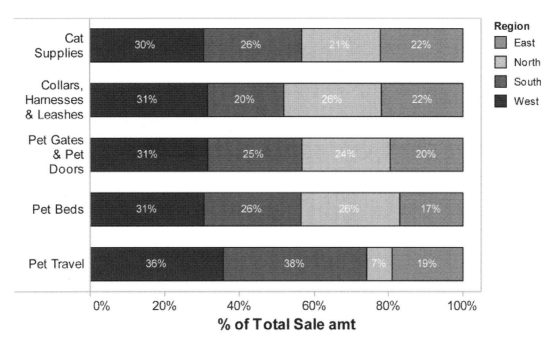

Now you can easily compare all five product lines, as well as see the contributions of even the smallest product line. The highest contribution of sales of any product line and region is *Pet Travel* in the South, although overall this product line is not that successful.

151

Stacked bar charts can be quite complex, so here's a quick synopsis of the uses that we've shown here:

Actual values
— overall distribution of primary category
— some idea of secondary category

Relative values
— for easier comparison, label the percent contribution made by secondary category
— take it up a notch by changing the metric to percent contribution which makes the large bars identical in height, so it's even easier to compare

Expert tips

- Only stack sums or counts—don't stack averages, because stacking a bunch of averages is not only confusing, it is also very misleading.

- For maximum impact, place the three stacked bar chart types on one slide or page.

- If you only have a small space, such as a one-page summary report, consider a stacked bar chart instead of multiple bar or pie charts, since it is much more compact.

Visually comparing members of the secondary category may be quicker with an *area chart*, an advanced chart type that is common in the popular media.

For example, look at this stacked bar chart. While you can easily compare the heights of the whole bars to see the overall changes in the primary category (total sales) over the 6-month period, it's difficult to compare the individual stacks between bars to follow the changes in the secondary category (region). Instead, you tend to look at the stacks in each bar individually.

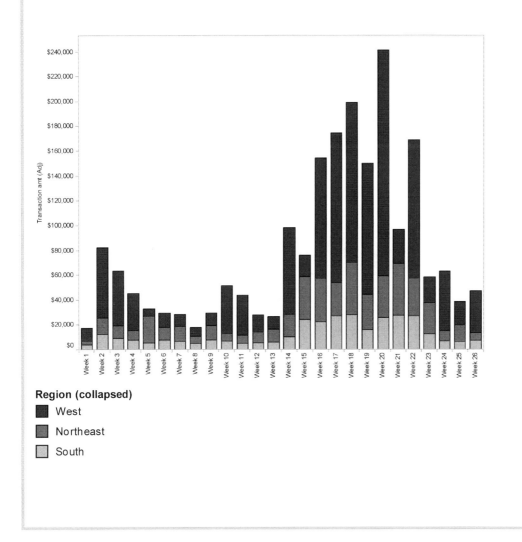

Region (collapsed)
- West
- Northeast
- South

153

Now, take a look at the area chart on the next page. Because the area is continuous and not split into separate bars, it is easier to study what happened in the secondary category (region) over time.

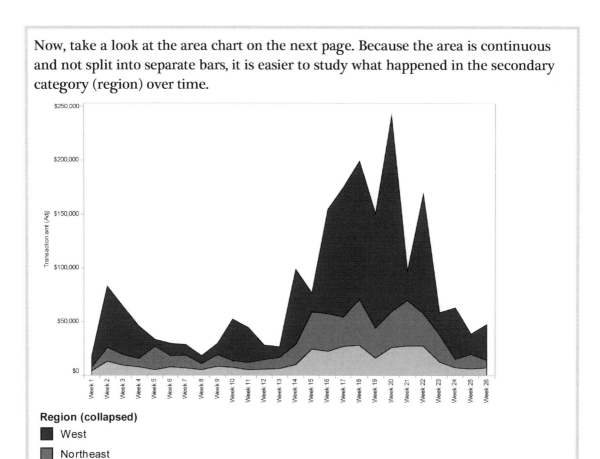

Region (collapsed)
- West
- Northeast
- South

Pitfalls

- It can be difficult to compare very small stacks.

- Don't overdo it with the stacks! Use no more than 6-8 stacks, and group the rest into "Other", similar to what we recommended with pie charts.

- If you must use many stacks and it's hard to read, consider a *line chart* with a different color line for each value. This is especially useful for looking at data changes over time. Line charts are covered later in this C.

Bar chart with related metric
displayed in shading (or color)

If you would like to see the intensity or range of a second related metric on each bar, use a bar chart with related metric in shading (or color, if you are able to use it). The first metric is still represented by size (the height or length of the bar).

For example, suppose you would like to examine how merchandise returns affect profit for your top eight product lines. You create a bar chart, where the length of the bar represents profit, and add a related metric in shading, which is the percentage that returns decreased profit.

**The length of the bars shows profit,
while shading shows how merchandise returns reduce profit**

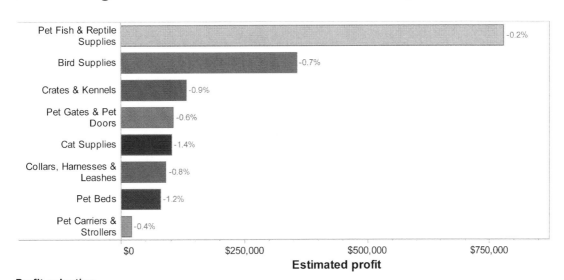

The darker the bar, the more returns cut into profit, so the product line with the highest percentage of loss due to returns is *Cat Supplies*. Notice how the darker bars stand out against the white background.

155

Remember that this doesn't mean *Cat Supplies* returns cause the highest decrease in profit in <u>dollar amount</u>. The most profitable product line, *Pet Fish & Reptile Supplies*, has the lowest percentage of profit loss due to returns, but loses more money.

Expert tips

- This is one more alternative to the multi-pane bar chart.

- Make sure that the shading or colors reflect your message, as discussed in the highlight table section.

- These are also useful to show performance relative to plan.

Pitfalls

- Try not to confuse your audience by adding a metric in shading or color that is not directly related to the current problem. A good test is: "Does this metric help to me answer this question?"

- If you do need to add an unrelated metric, clearly define this in the title or the color legend.

- People often use the bar chart with metric in shading (or color) when they really need the details of a table or highlight table. Instead, show a basic bar chart along with the detailed table.

Side-by-side bar charts are used to compare related metrics side-by-side in the pane of a graph.

These are not used that much because people often find them hard to read.

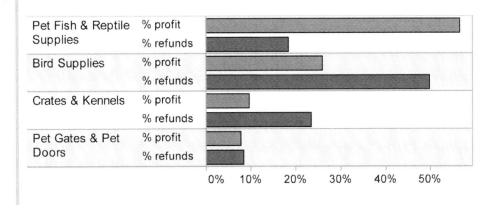

Circle plots

If your bar chart isn't displaying the details of the data that you need, a *circle plot* can help take it up a notch. It's similar to a bar chart, but the circles allow you to show more details instead of only the overall sum or average.

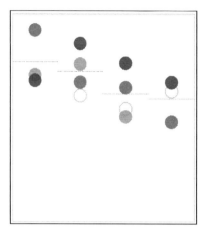

You are interested in finding out if certain types of customers have more returns than others. The customers are divided into four *customer segments*, the primary category, which are groups based on buying behavior, lifestyle and demographic data. They are also divided according to the region where they live, the secondary category. What are the average refund amounts for customers by segment and region?

Need more than just the overall average?
Show more detailed averages

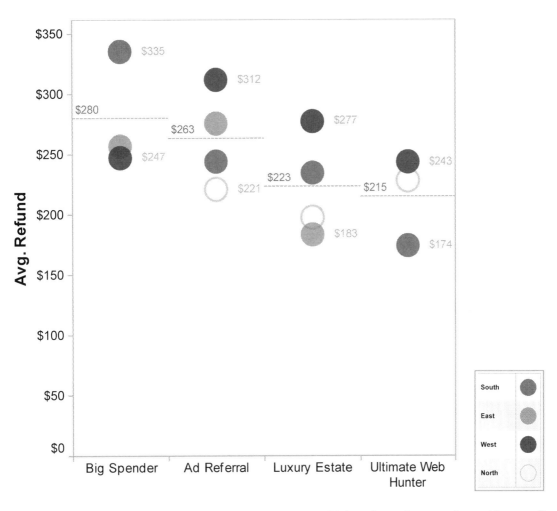

If this were a bar chart, the tops of the bars would be the reference lines (the small horizontal lines) marked with the overall averages, such as $280 for *Big Spender*. The primary category, customer segment, is sorted by descending average refund amounts.

In the circle plot, you can also see average refund for specific groups of customers, so you can ask detailed questions. Where do the *Ad Referral* customers with the highest average refund amount live? The dark, filled-in circle at the top is the South (as shown in the legend) and the amount is $312. Who has the lowest average refund amount? *Ultimate web hunters* who live in the East have the lowest at $174.

This is a very powerful chart type that is underutilized, especially if additional details beyond a bar chart would be valuable.

Expert tips

- It is often a good enhancement to add a reference line showing either the average or median for the primary category.

- If the circles are numerous or overlapping, consider using open circles or plus signs instead of the colored circles for clarity.

- Circle plots are more compact than multi-pane bar charts.

- Unlike stacked bar charts, you can show the average values of the various groups of the secondary category.

Pitfalls

- These might take your audience by surprise since they are new to most people.

- If your circles represent sums (such as sales by region), the reference line needs to point out the average of the sums. If you want to emphasize the grand total instead, opt for a stacked bar chart.

- Be careful of how your analysis software calculates the average. If the circles represent averages, the software will likely display the average of averages, instead of a weighted average (see *Heads Up* box below). This may be misleading. You might need to calculate the weighted average, or program your software to do it, and add the correct value yourself.

Heads Up

The average of averages can be very different from the weighted average. If you have three values that represent the average sale amounts in each of three states, such as $10, $20, and $30, the average of those averages is **$20** (the sum, $60, divided by 3). But what if there are only 1,000 customers in the first 2 states, and 10,000 in the 3rd?

A weighted average, in which the number of customers is taken into account, would be useful. First, calculate this amount: ($10 X 1,000 customers) + ($20 X 1,000) + ($30 X 10,000) = 330,000. Then divide this by 12,000, the total number of customers (1,000 + 1,000 + 10,000) for the weighted average, which equals **$27.50**. A far cry from $20!

---

choose
questions

collect

data

check

clean

chart

analysis

custom

communicate

results

FYI

You may need to understand the contribution of individual members of a category to the value of a metric and especially the importance of the top members in painting the entire picture.

Pareto charts are useful for this. Do some research if you plan to use them, but here is a quick introduction. In the example below, Customer IDs are on the horizontal axis, Sales are bars and measured on the left axis, and % of Cumulative Sales is the line and measured on the right axis. While your company might have 5000 customers, you can easily examine how many make up the majority of your total sales. The top 16% of customers account for 50% of all company sales. This is important to know when making decisions, since you may want to make certain decisions based only on your best customers.

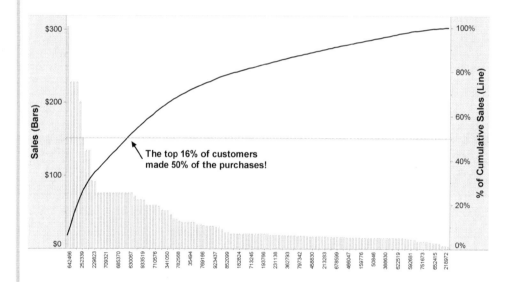

Pareto charts were created to display the **80/20 rule**. The original idea was from Vilfredo Pareto, an Italian economist in the 1900s, who observed that 80% of the land in Italy was owned by 20% of its citizens. It has been applied to many different scenarios, such as 80% of the profit comes from 20% of the customers, or 80% of customer complaints come from 20% of the customers.

SCENARIO #4. TIME TRAVEL:
EXAMINE HOW YOUR DATA CHANGE OVER TIME

Business questions often deal with how circumstances change over time. In this scenario, we demonstrate how to investigate changes over time with *basic line charts* and *dual-axis line charts*.

Basic line charts

If you would like to investigate how a data item or multiple data items changed over a period of time, use a *basic line chart*, also referred to as a *growth rate chart* or *time series*.

How many customers placed orders each month during 2010 and 2011?

You graph the data in a basic line chart.

**Shows the overall trend and
max and min for number of customers over time**

Time is on the horizontal or **x-axis**, and the data item that you are tracking over time (here *Customers ordering per month*) is on the vertical axis or **y-axis**. This chart is called a *continuous* line chart because there are no breaks in the line, and is useful to observe the long-term trends and volatility in the data. For instance, the overall trend increases and peaks in mid-2011, and then plummets. There is also a spike in number of customers in Q2 of 2010. It's also helpful to label the maximum and minimum.

Discrete line chart

The same data are now shown in a *discrete* line chart.

Easier to compare specific time periods:
Q3 in 2010 versus 2011?

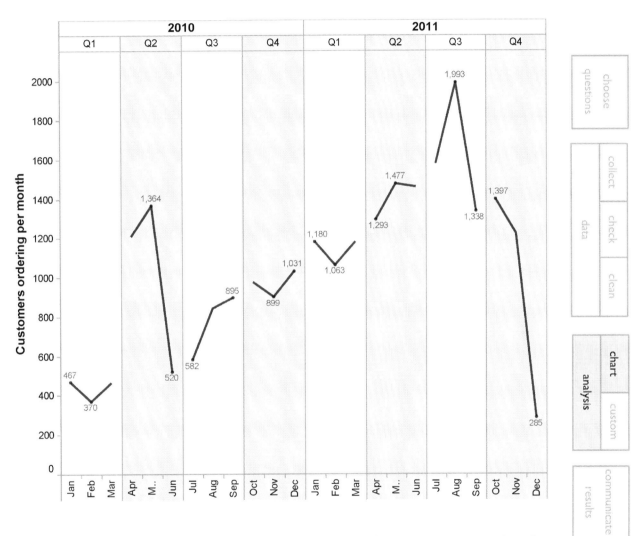

The discrete line chart divides your data into blocks of time for easy comparison of similar time periods. For instance, compare Q1 for the first year to Q1 in the second year. The shape of the line represents the behavior of the data item during that time period. Are the shapes of the line the same or different? The direction of the line represents if there was growth or decline. Do the lines go up or down?

Helpful Hint

Many people do not like the discrete line chart at first, because they are used to the traditional continuous line chart.

Give it a shot, as you may realize that it is easier for you quickly find information when you are in a rush.

Get ready—we are chock-full of advice for this graph type.

Expert tips

- Show the zero-axis. Otherwise the graph may imply a misleading growth rate, by making it appear that there was a lot of growth or shrinkage, when there wasn't. The exception to this is if the area of interest is volatile or variable.

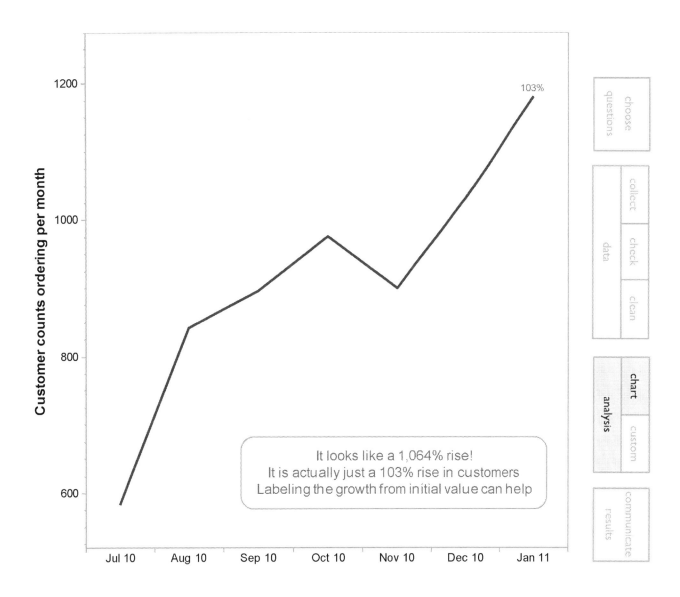

- For easier comparison of multiple years on the same chart, use different colors for different lines.

- Stick with simple line types, and avoid dashes and dots.

- It's useful to have a point of reference on a line graph. Label the minimum and maximum values or the beginning and ending values on your line.

- If the data are highly volatile on a daily basis, instead of showing every data point, average or sum by month for an easier-to-read chart.

- If you need to know the amount of something to date rather than just individual values, consider using a *running total*. *Year-to-date* is a typical one.

- Use multi-pane line charts when appropriate. They are similar to multi-pane bar charts, but are aligned with a continuous metric instead of a categorical data item (see *Scenario #5, Was it worth the money?*).

To make it easier to see percent growth from baseline (the first value), use an **index**.

Index values or numbers are commonly used to study a metric over time. In this context, the baseline refers to a value at a particular time period, such as a day, month, quarter or year. For instance, if you sold 150 dog parkas on January 1st, that would be the daily baseline. The baseline is assigned an index value of 100, which is the value typically used by analysts. Numbers of parkas sold above 150 are represented by index numbers above 100, and numbers of parkas sold below 150 are represented by index numbers below 100.

If you sold 75 dog parkas on February 1st, the index value for that date would be **50**:

(75 dog parkas on February 1st / 150 dog parkas on January 1st) X 100 = 50

If you'd like to know how the percentage growth in sales of dog parkas differs between the two dates, subtract 100 from the index number of the date that you are comparing to the baseline:

50 – 100 = -50, or you sold 50% fewer parkas on February 1st compared to January 1st

For more details on how to calculate index, consult a statistical reference.

choose questions

collect data
check
clean

analysis
chart
custom

communicate results

169

Pitfalls

- Line charts can be used for other data besides date data, such as to show a profit margin or discount rate over time. However, be careful not to draw a line between data points that shouldn't be connected, because it implies that there's a relationship when there's not. For instance, sales on Monday are related to sales on Tuesday, since they are sequential days, so it is okay to connect them. Pajamas sales are not directly or obviously related to shoe sales, so they shouldn't be connected.

- Labeling every value on the line can clutter the graph. For easy look-up of the details, insert a table beside the graph with dates and values.

FYI

You may have heard the term **forecasting**, often with regards to future growth.

Basic forecasting is an analytical method where you can use historical data to paint a picture of what may happen to your business in the future. If you are interested, appropriate software tools include Forecast Pro, SAS, JMP, SPSS, and R.

Heads Up

Drawing a **regression line** on a line chart doesn't make it a forecast.

If you've done this, you know what we're talking about. The details can be found in a statistics book, but simple regression only takes into account the overall direction of the data in recent months. It doesn't include seasonality or auto-regression. For instance, sales today are often affected by several factors such as sales yesterday, sales the same day last month, or sales the same day last year.

Dual-axis line charts

If you are trying to compare two quantitative metrics that are related to other, yet have different scales or units of measurement, a *dual-axis line chart* is an option. These are also called *dual-scaled axis graphs*.

For instance, you may want to compare two metrics that have the same units, but different scales. A common example of this is comparing sales with profit, which are both in dollars. Typically, sales will be much higher than profit, so profit would be hard to read using the same metric (unless you are fortunate enough to be in a business where almost all sales dollars are profit).

You are looking into customer refunds by month since January 2010. How do sales and refunds compare? First, you create two basic line charts: one of sales over time and one of refunds over time (don't worry if you can't read the axes—that's not the point of this illustration).

Hard to compare sales with refunds in two separate charts

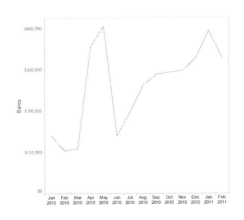 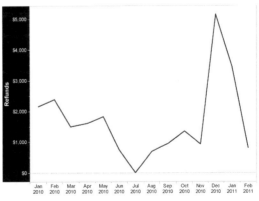

You have to go back and forth between the two graphs to figure out what's going on, and it's not working very well. If all this information was on a single graph, that would be useful. You then combine these two into one dual-axis line chart.

Although the data are erratic, this chart is easier for comparisons

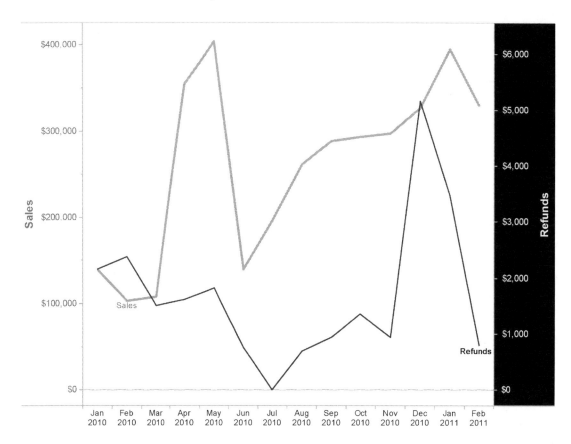

The "dual" or two axes are vertical, or y-axes, and time is on the horizontal or x-axis. Sales are on the left y-axis and represented by the gray line, and refunds are on the right y-axis and represented by the black line. This view type is useful to see both the actual values of the two metrics, as well as the relative growth of the two metrics.

Although both lines are highly variable (much like data in the real world), in general in 2010, there is a lag of refunds increasing about one month past sales peaking. You would expect this; more sales lead to more returns in the near future. However, July 2010 is surprising, because refunds were $0. Maybe you should see if there's a data problem? Finally, there's a surge in refunds in December 2010.

When looking at a dual-axis line chart, if you need a place to start, the two questions to ask are:
1. Is one metric growing faster than the other?
2. Is one metric changing direction (increasing or decreasing) at a different time than the other?

Expert tips

- Both lines should start at the same point on the chart, as shown in the illustration, which can be done by adjusting one of the axes up or down. This makes it easier to compare the growth of either data item at any date against the baseline.

- For each line, it may be useful to label the start, the minimum and the maximum. This will call attention to the different scales on each axis, as well as provide details.

- To make it obvious which line is which, use a different color for each line (or shade for black-and-white) and make axis headers match their respective line colors.

- Instead of using a dual-axis line chart, you may want to use *multi-pane **line** charts* with the two metrics (see *Scenario #5, Was it worth the money?*), which are similar to the multi-pane bar charts previously described.

- See basic line charts for more tips.

FYI

Dual-axis, bar-line charts are similar to dual-axis, line-line charts.

They are used in Pareto charts, shown in an FYI box in *Scenario #3, Extreme Comparisons* and to calculate ROI, in *Scenario #5, Was it worth the money?*

choose questions

collect

check

clean

data

chart

analysis

custom

communicate

results

Pitfalls

- What does it mean when the two lines intersect?

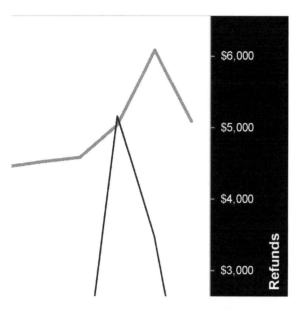

- Nothing! People naturally focus on the intersection, assuming it has a meaning. However, if *you* have aligned the starting points of the two lines, these intersections are where the growth is identical, which might be meaningful.

- The purpose of the dual axes is defeated if you force the two axes to synchronize with each other, because then you wind up with the same scale on each axis, regardless if the values are one million on one axis and one thousand on the other.

- See basic line charts for more Pitfalls.

FYI

Dual-axis line charts are somewhat controversial.

Some experts argue that they shouldn't be used at all, or should only be used to compare different units, not different scales of the same unit.

174

SCENARIO #5. WAS IT WORTH THE MONEY?
DETERMINE RETURN ON INVESTMENT (ROI)

In this scenario, we demonstrate a basic example of how to assess if your investment paid off using a **multi-pane line chart** and a **bar-line chart**.

Multi-pane line charts

These are useful if you are looking at multiple metrics over time. They are similar to multi-pane bar charts, except they have two or more *line charts* in panes that make up a larger overall chart. Also, they typically are aligned using a continuous metric like date instead of being subdivided by a categorical data item.

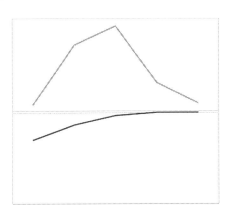

For example, you ran an ad campaign to promote your *Pet Houses* product line for three months in 2010: May, June, and July. You want to know if the campaign boosted profit in those three months, and then in August and September, past the duration of the campaign.

The monthly cost of the campaign varied depending on how many web ads were displayed and which newspapers ran your banner ad. This cost is shown in the bottom pane of this illustration. Gross profit is sales revenue less the cost to the company of the products sold. So, gross profit earned on the additional pet houses sold or attributed to the ad campaign is displayed in the top pane.

175

Multi-pane line chart with gross profit and ad costs aligned by month

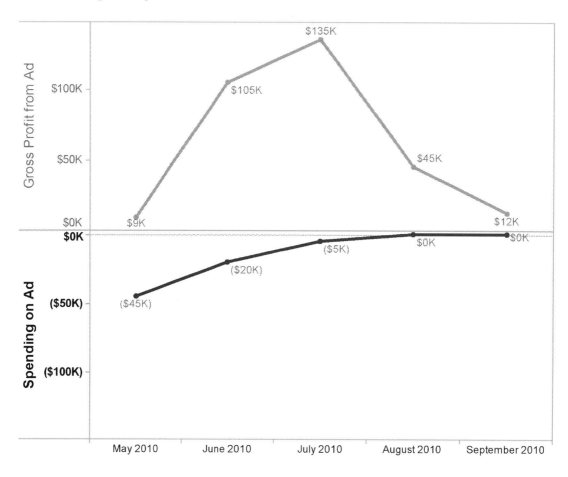

This chart allows you to place the negative values below the zero-axis (spending on ad) and the positive values above the zero-axis (gross profit from ad) so you can easily compare the metrics with each other on a monthly basis. You can use amounts for profit and spending from this chart to determine return on investment (ROI).

For example, **ROI through July is:**

ROI = *(Cumulative Gross Profit – Cumulative Spending) / Cumulative Spending*

ROI = ($9K + $105K + $135K) – ($45K + $20K + $5K) / ($45K + $20K + $5K)

ROI = <u>255%</u>

May through July was a success.

What if you'd like to see ROI for May through September? Try the next graph type.

Bar-line charts

These are another type of dual-axis chart, with one metric represented by bars and the second represented by a line.

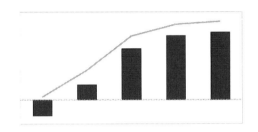

In the next illustration, the bottom pane is the *cumulative* or running total of what was spent on the ad campaign, so each month is the sum of that month plus all previous months. The top pane is a bar-line chart, with the bars representing cumulative ROI, and the line representing cumulative gross profit.

177

Bar-line charts are useful for cumulative or running totals of two different metrics

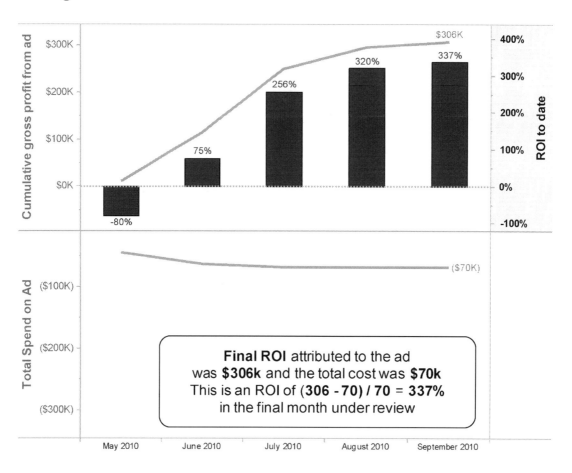

The final ROI for the whole campaign is:

ROI = ($306,000 - $70,000) / $70,000

ROI = 337%

Great investment!

Expert tips

- This is a brief introduction to a basic method for calculating ROI. In the real world, it can get quite complicated, and companies and even departments within the same company calculate it differently.

- Often, the exact ROI is not important, but analysts use it to evaluate various alternatives.

- Dual-axis, bar-line charts are useful for ROI analysis, because you can see revenue and ROI (and in the last example, spending) over different time periods in the same view.

Helpful Hint

Adding comments to your chart or tagging data points can draw attention to useful information, and help others understand the chart if you're not there.

These have various names, such as *caption, tooltip, label, annotation,* or *hover values.*

Heads Up

Dual-axis, bar-line charts can be misleading in two ways:

1. The data item represented by the bars is overemphasized, simply because the bars take up a lot more area of the view than does the line.
2. They imply that the bar is a discrete data item and the line is a continuous data item.

However, they are used in Pareto charts (shown in *Scenario #3. Extreme Comparisons*), in addition to ROI analysis.

choose questions

collect data
check
clean

chart
analysis
custom

communicate results

Pitfalls

- Estimating what proportion of sales can be tied to a marketing campaign usually requires an experienced analyst.

- The sales data are often located in a totally different place from the data regarding what was spent on the marketing campaign—sometimes it's even in a contract with a marketing firm or other form, so it has to be manually entered.

SCENARIO #6. DID I MEASURE UP?
REACH YOUR GOAL

In this section, we discuss *bullet graphs*, which allow fast review of performance relative to your goals. There's a good chance you haven't seen one of these before, since it's a relatively new chart type.

Bullet graphs

If you would like to evaluate how close you've come to attaining a goal, use a bullet graph, an enhanced version of a standard bar chart.

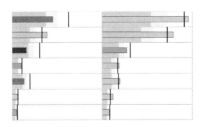

A bullet graph displays the actual and target values for each category, allowing you to review how close the actual values are to the target values.

How close did the company come to reaching sales targets for each product line in 2010? Use a bullet graph. The horizontal bar represents the "bullet", in this case the actual sales, and the small vertical line (also called a reference line) is the target, which in this case is a sales target.

Did you come close to your sales targets?

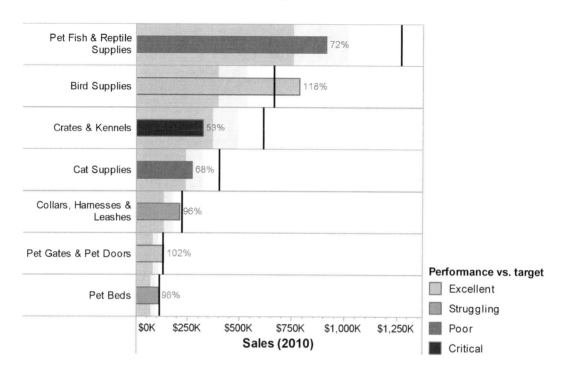

We added some finishing touches to this bullet graph. Look at the legend that describes the shading of the horizontal bars—the darker the bar, the worse the actual sales relative to the target. So, sales of *Crates & Kennels* really missed the target, while *Bird Supplies* sales hit the ball out of the park.

Expert tips

- Bullet graphs enable the review of a lot of information in a compact area, so they are a wonderful way to review many items in a limited space.

- Bullet graphs are a great alternative to using dashboard gauges or meters to assess goals. Gauges and meters are disliked by many experts since they are difficult to read and interpret. In contrast, bullet charts can easily show many categories at the same time while allowing quick review.

- Sort the bars in descending order, either by target or actual values, depending on which you would like to emphasize.

- Consider shading or color-coding the bullet, or bar, to show how close the actual values are to the target values: the brighter the color, the farther away from the target, which draws people's attention to potential problem areas.

Pitfalls

- People unfamiliar with bullet graphs usually require a brief explanation and a few minutes to understand them. Sharing how the chart works and how they can be quickly reviewed will help with broad adoption across your team.

- Verify that the target and the actual values have not been flipped in the graph. Actual outcomes are the bars (bullets) and the target is the reference line.

- If the target value is for the whole year, and the actual value is only year-to-date, you will likely be way off target—but this is not an accurate picture. Adjust your target for the value expected at this time of the year, realizing that this may not be a simple proportional adjustment. For instance, you may make half your annual sales in the last quarter of the year due to the holidays.

FYI

If your company deals primarily with extremely large sales that occur infrequently, such as a construction company or real estate, you may need to use a more specialized chart type for goal attainment, such as a **sales pipeline**.

If you are interested in this unusual case, consult a reference that focuses on sales analysis.

SCENARIO #7. LITTLE THINGS ADD UP: GRAPH CUMULATIVE RESULTS

In this section, we describe how to graph cumulative results on *line charts with running totals or year-to-date (YTD) totals.*

Line charts with running or YTD totals

This is a variation of a basic line chart which clearly displays cumulative results over time.

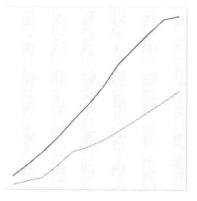

You'd like to examine sales over time for 2010 versus 2011. However, you're not sure which is better: a line chart with YTD sales totals or a basic line chart that simply shows sales by month.

First, you graph cumulative sales totals on a line chart. This is an easy way to compare cumulative results across 2010 and 2011. This shows the running total on a monthly basis.

Line chart with year-to-date sales
is great for comparing different years

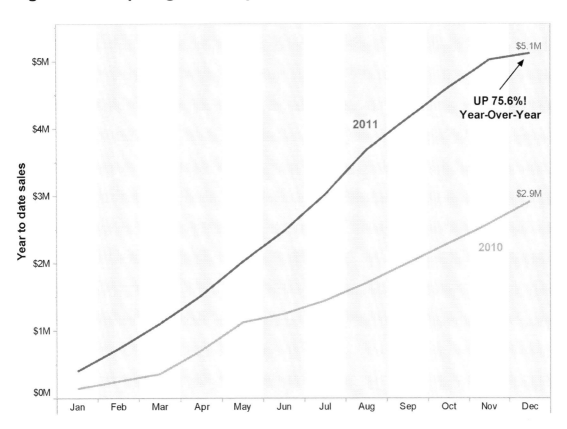

Year-over-year total sales in 2011 were up 76% compared to 2010. There's also a noticeable slowing in sales in May 2010.

Next, you put sales by month on a basic line chart.

**Line chart with monthly sales shows
details of what happened throughout the year
(maxes and mins labeled)**

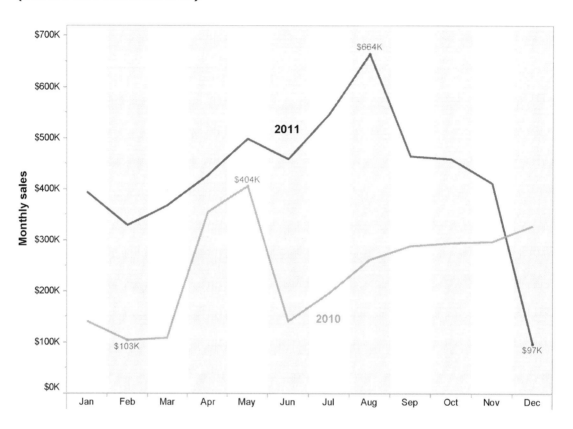

How does this compare to the line chart with cumulative sales? The question at hand should determine which one to use.

1. The huge drop-off in late 2011 is clear in the monthly chart, while not apparent in the cumulative line chart. Notice that the cumulative results graph will deemphasize or even mask changes in sales, especially later in the year.

2. Conversely, it is obvious in the cumulative line chart that 2011 is a vastly superior year overall versus 2010. However, if you only examine the cumulative line chart, you could miss a big problem that is rapidly occurring in the business.

Expert tips

- Cumulative results are best for understanding performance over long periods of time.

- When you show year-to-date data, prepare the same period for the previous year as a reference. You can do this by filtering last year through the same month and day as the current day of this year.

Pitfalls

- Cumulative results can mask problems that are best displayed in monthly or weekly increments, because they can mask subtle or recent problems in short time periods.

- Adjust your year-to-date amounts based on your business; for instance, if you get most of your business in the last quarter, take this into account.

- Be careful not to sum up percentages, ratios or averages.

187

SCENARIO #8. WHERE THE ACTION IS: MAP YOUR DATA

In this scenario, we explain the basics of using maps.

If location is crucial to the problem that you are investigating, display your key metrics on *maps*.

What is the average sale amount by state? You start with a bar chart.

A list of states is not very interesting and hard to read

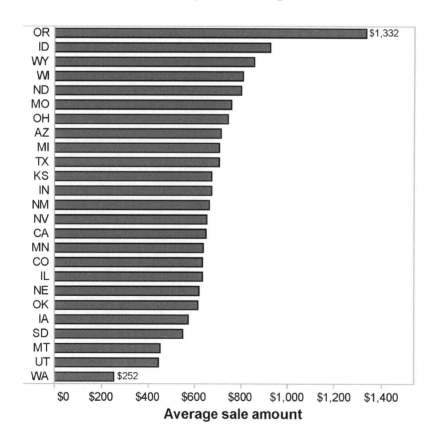

Since you're interested in locations, a map would be more interesting.

Sales data by state looks good on a map

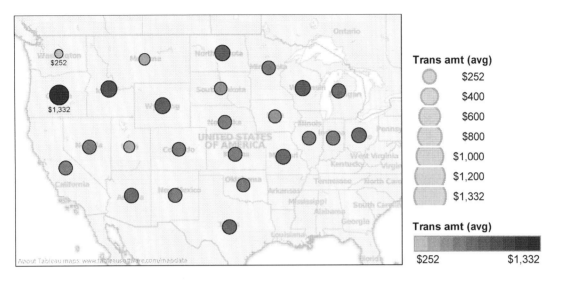

The average transaction amount is **double-encoded** on the map. This means that it is displayed in two ways, by bubble size and shading (or color intensity) in this view, for emphasis. Notice that it's easy to pick out the states with the highest and lowest average transaction amount, Oregon and Washington respectively, which are also labeled with the values. It is interesting that the amount is five times higher in Oregon than Washington, because these two states are alike in many ways: they are adjacent, on the coast, contain mountains, and offer similar lifestyles.

What if you wanted to quickly find the five top or bottom states? Symbols can be useful on maps.

189

It's easy to pick out the best and the worst

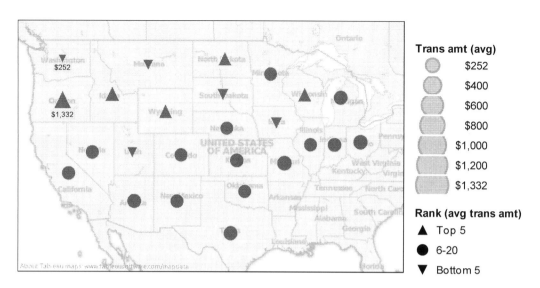

Until recently, mapping was quite technical, so most likely an accidental analyst wouldn't have done much of it. However, it's become more accessible with newer software. Since maps have recently become popular in everyday analysis, we have many tips on how to create them.

Expert tips

- When you have a lot of detail, show subsets of the maps, either by breaking up the presentation into parts or using an interactive mapping tool. For instance, if you have four regional managers, and you want to display sales by zip code, break down the sales into four maps, one for the territory of each manager, instead of one big U.S. map that makes the details hard to find.

- Supplement the map by placing relevant data in another chart type. For the previous example, you may want to display sales for each state in a circle plot or bullet graph below the map.

- Use space efficiently:
    - If you have U.S. data from all 50 states, there is a lot of space between Alaska or Hawaii and the mainland, so use a second inset map for those two states.
    - If you only have data for California, for example, just show California, not the whole U.S.

- For world maps, show summaries for continents or regions rather than displaying data for every country.

Pitfalls

- Using filled maps may misrepresent the data. In a filled map, entire states or regions are shaded to display the intensity of a metric such as high versus low sales.

- For example, sales are much higher in Rhode Island and Washington DC than the neighboring states of New York and Maryland. On a map, you fill in Rhode Island and Washington DC with a dark shade and New York and Maryland with a lighter shade, However, New York and Maryland appear to have higher sales simply because they are much bigger states, and comprise a much larger area in the map.

-

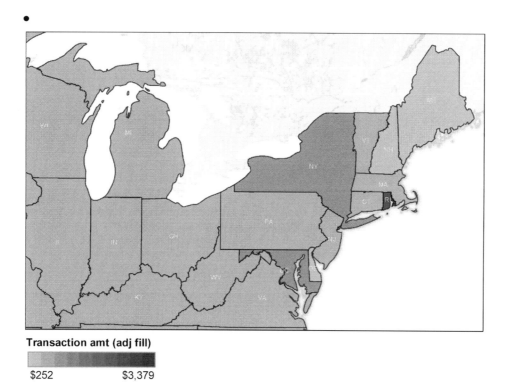

Transaction amt (adj fill)

$252 $3,379

- A better option is to display circles over each location that encode intensity by size. This places small locations on an even playing field with larger ones.

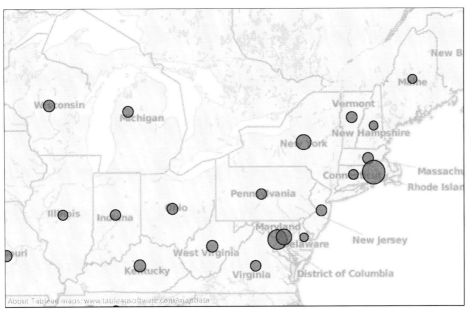

Transaction amt (adj fill)

○	$252
●	$1,000
●	$2,000
●	$3,379

- Avoid cluttering your map with excessive labels:

  — Instead of showing every location with a label, show only the minimum and maximum location values, perhaps by region.

  — In place of actual amounts, it may be appropriate to show rankings. If there are 8.425 million people in your largest city and 7.163 million in your second largest, replace these numbers with a simple ranking of "1" and "2" (we cover ranking in detail in *The Sixth C: Customize Your Analysis*).

  — If you have data at the state level, putting county and city names on the map may distract people from or obscure the important information. It can also confuse people into thinking that you have more detailed data than are displayed.

- Similar to the pie chart, if you have negative values, you can't size-encode the data, because how can you have a negative size? Use color or shading instead. For example, the shading could diverge from red to green, to show negative to positive values.

SCENARIO #9. THE STORY IS IN THE DETAILS: EXPAND THE DETAILS OF IMPORTANT DATA ITEMS

This scenario is different from the previous ones, because we are not introducing a chart type. If high-level or grouped data are not giving you the details you need to answer your questions, expand the relevant data items.

You may discover a lot of information by simply "drilling down" into high-level values to see more detailed information. If you would like to find out where to send a postcard mailing about an upcoming sale, sales data by region isn't detailed enough to help you.

Is region too general? Drill down to state and zip code

Drilling into the details of a data item can be thought of as a simple type of filtering. You are likely familiar with this concept from shopping on the internet. For example, you would like to shop for women's red high-heeled shoes on Amazon. You select

Clothing, Shoes and Jewelry → Shoes → Women → Pumps → Color (Red) →
Shoe Shape (Pump Shape).

Each click brings you down to the next, more specific level of detail, until you've arrived at a specific level of interest.

Expanding the details of a data item can be used as a multipurpose tool, because it can solve a variety of business problems.

Location: Country → State → City → Zip Code → Zip + 4

Sales Region: Region → District → Territory

Date: Year → Quarter → Month → Day
                               or
                               Fiscal Year → Fiscal Quarter → Fiscal Week → Day of Week

---

Helpful Hint

For more advanced filtering techniques, look in *The Sixth C: Customize Your Analysis.*

Expert tips

- "Layer" your presentation or report to show the logic behind your drill-down. Perhaps your audience is familiar with sales by product line, so start there if you are showing some interesting observations two levels down. This will give them a context that they can understand.

- This technique can be useful in presentations, but typically is for you to analyze the data at your desk. If you find something very important with this technique, you should consider the best way to present the finding in a table or graph.

Pitfalls

- It can be easy to forget that you have drilled down to a more detailed level, and you may analyze the data later thinking you have the entire dataset. Instead, you are using only a subset of the data.

Bonus Scenario: Frequency of Occurrences

Counting the frequency of occurrences is a useful tool, but it is often overlooked in business. A *histogram* is useful for frequency counts. Research this more if you would like to use histograms, but here is a basic example. Count of products is on the vertical axis and warranty length is on the horizontal axis. For example, about 500 products have no warranty.

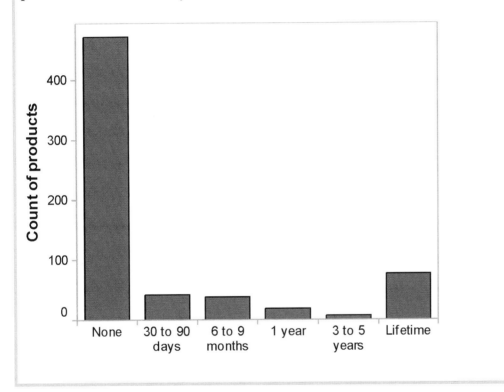

FYI

Another Bonus Scenario: Relationships

Determining the relationship of two related metrics can be useful. A *scatter plot* can depict this.

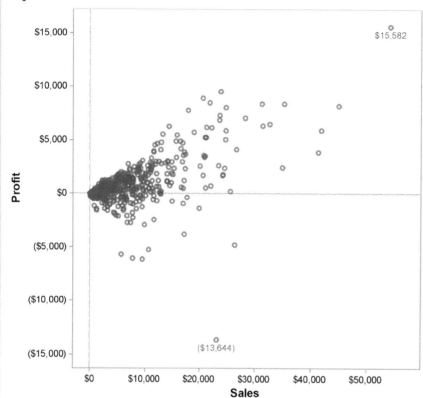

Be careful not to assume that one metric causes the pattern in the other.

We cover relationships in more detail in *The Sixth C: Customize Your Analysis.*

SCENARIO #10. TRY, TRY AGAIN: REVISIT THE QUESTION IF YOU DIDN'T GET IT RIGHT THE FIRST TIME

*The trouble with doing something right the first time
is that nobody appreciates how difficult it was.*

—UNKNOWN

At the end of your analysis, you may need to spend a few minutes on a "reality check".

Did you answer your question?

It's easy to get so wrapped up in the data and analysis techniques that you lose sight of your goal, and wind up answering the wrong question, or worse, no question at all!

To give you an idea of what we're referring to, here are a few of the most common situations where people think that they are done with their analyses, but they didn't quite make it to the finish line.

Insufficient context

You begin your analysis to investigate whether sales have grown this quarter, but you end up showing only the sales figures for this quarter. You haven't provided sufficient context to easily answer the question, since you can't assume your audience knows what the previous quarter looks like. You should show the sales figures for the previous quarters, including the same quarter last year and possibly even the year before that. Be creative with this, by displaying year-over-year growth if you don't want to show the values separately. You could also show the results versus planned, forecasted, or budgeted amounts.

Information overload

You have provided a lot of analysis results, including many details. You review it, and realize you've buried the answers in too much information, and it's hard to make any decisions. This is a common mistake, because people often have a hard time separating out the relevant results from the irrelevant, especially if they've spent a lot of time on the analysis.

For example, your manager wants you to make a recommendation on how to spend the remaining 3% of the quarterly marketing budget. You show lots of details about every ad bought and order placed, and all the possible ways to spend the remaining portion of the budget. You definitely went too far! Show a summary of the remaining money, the top five ways to spend it, and your choice with estimated payback.

Lack of relevant information

You would like to assess how your company is doing this year. Sales are great, doubling versus the same period last year. However, you overlook that the sales of your nearest competitor quadrupled. This could be a large oversight, because great sales for your company may still be bad in the marketplace, where you're losing market share. One warning: using external data in a large presentation should first be reviewed with your boss. There can be hot-button issues hidden here that require diplomacy.

Helpful Hint

It's okay to go back to previous C's if you realize that you need a new question, different data or to create another chart.

Just be careful not to skip important steps along the way, such as cleaning up the new data.

Expect the unexpected:
Sometimes there's no clear answer or you're totally surprised by the results

The most exciting phrase to hear in science,
the one that heralds new discoveries,
is not 'Eureka!' ('I found it!')
but rather 'hmm....that's funny...'

—ISAAC ASIMOV
American science fiction author and biochemist

Hopefully, after charting your data, you are able to come up with a clear answer to what actions you should take to address your business problem. However, we would like to address a result that will likely happen to you at some point, and it's one of the most frustrating parts of being an analyst.

For example, you give your customers a free pair of pet sunglasses with their purchase. You are trying to figure out if they would prefer a pet baseball cap. You spent a lot of time prepping your data. You came up with a fabulous analysis and you can't wait to see the results.

Then you are confused by inconclusive results. The data vary too much and there is not enough of a clear difference to come up with a definite decision. Be careful not to read more than what is there.

Alternatively, you come up with totally unexpected results that don't make any sense. If you feel relatively confident in them, investigate further. You may find out information that you would never have predicted, but on which you can take action to help you accomplish your goals.

RECAP OF THE FIFTH C: CHART YOUR ANALYSIS

	BUSINESS SCENARIO	TAKE ACTION
1	*When precision matters* Compare exact values	Tables Highlight tables *FYI box:* Heat maps
2	*Winners and losers* Compare different categories at a glance	Basic bar charts Multi-pane bar charts Pie charts (also see Highlight tables and Heat maps)
3	*Extreme comparisons* Go beyond basic bar charts to compare between and within categories	Stacked bar charts *FYI box:* Area charts Bar charts with related metric displayed in shading (or color) *FYI box:* Side-by-side bar charts Circle plots *FYI box:* Pareto charts
4	*Time travel* Examine how your data change over time	Basic line charts Dual-axis line charts (also see Multi-pane line charts)
5	*Was it worth the money?* Determine Return on Investment (ROI)	Multi-pane line charts Bar-line charts (also see Scatter plot)

	BUSINESS SCENARIO	TAKE ACTION
6	*Did I measure up?* Reach your goal	Bullet graphs (also see Dual-axis line charts and Maps)
7	*Little things add up* Graph cumulative results	Line chart with running or YTD totals
8	*Where the action is* Map your data	Maps
9	*The story is in the details* Expand the details of important data items	Add captions to your chart to point out useful information Display the data shown in your chart in a cross-tab, pivot table, or detailed listing
Bonus	*Frequency of occurrences*	*FYI box:* Histogram
Bonus	*Relationships*	*FYI box:* Scatter plot
10	*Try, try again* Revisit the question if you didn't get it right the first time	Mix and match chart types

choose
questions

collect
data

check

clean

analysis

chart

custom

communicate
results

Now you can move on to *The Sixth C: Customize Your Analysis*, where you'll learn simple and flexible techniques that are invaluable for taking your analysis "to the next level".

We end this chapter with another quote from the famous (and apparently witty) American statistician, John Tukey:

> *If you display information the right way,*
> *anybody can be an analyst.*

THE SIXTH C:
CUSTOMIZE YOUR ANALYSIS

All parts should go together without forcing.
You must remember that the parts you are reassembling
were disassembled by you.
Therefore, if you can't get them together again,
there must be a reason.
By all means, do not use a hammer.

—IBM MAINTENANCE MANUAL (1925)

Now that you've developed your visual analytic skills with the business scenarios shown in *The Fifth C: Chart Your Analysis*, you are ready for the next set of tools that will help you analyze and answer very specific problems. In *The Sixth C: Customize Your Analysis*, you will build upon the information from the previous C's. You will learn how to zero in on the right data using flexible techniques that can be done quickly, yet answer many common business questions.

In this C, we follow a real-world analyst in a multi-day, interactive meeting with her colleagues, as she analyzes the company data to answer their questions on the spot (which we like to refer to as "analyst on the hot seat"). We walk you through her thought processes as she interprets the questions, turning them into quick analyses that maximize the value of the data that she has immediately available to her. Just like anyone who analyzes data, she sometimes oversimplifies, misunderstands, or makes mistakes—but she focuses on improving her work. The "perfect" analysis rarely exists, but she is able to complete relevant, timely analyses that are useful to her colleagues.

Like The Fifth C, this C has a lot of detailed information. It will be a challenge to remember everything the first time around, so also use it as a reference.

In this case study, we use sales data and ask questions that should make sense to people from a wide range of backgrounds. Of course, you will probably answer different questions in this or other areas of business, but the point is to demonstrate the utility of flexible, simple data analysis. In the **Take-Home Message** boxes after each technique, we summarize how you can apply it in your line of work, including useful tips and tricks about analysis in general.

Note that some of the illustrations in this C are quite small. In these cases, the overall shape of the data is more important than the details.

COMPANY BACKGROUND

Maria is an analyst with a pet supply company. The company has a single "brick-and-mortar" flagship store, but most sales are made through the website, where you can communicate with a sales representative by either chatting online or calling the sales phone number. The company started out in 2000 by selling bird, fish, and reptile supplies, but in the last few years it has expanded into the lucrative dog and cat supply market.

Meeting Agenda

Over the next few days, Maria has a series of meetings with the five regional sales managers and their supervisor, the vice president (VP) of sales, to evaluate sales performance in the past two years, 2010 and 2011. The sales dataset contains 27,067 sales transactions, 20,172 customers, and supplemental information on returns and refunds.

Topic 1. Summary values: describe your data items in a nutshell

Topic 2. Sort your data: identify the major and minor players

Topic 3. Filter starter pack: utilize the power and flexibility of filters

Topic 4. Filters to set the dates: focus on a particular time period

Topic 5. Cascading filters: choose specific data with a series of filters

Topic 6. Right metric for the job: express metrics in the most informative way

Topic 7. Relationships: observe how one data item changes with another

Helpful Hint
A more detailed list is included for your reference in the recap at the end.

TOPIC 1. SUMMARY VALUES: DESCRIBE YOUR DATA ITEMS IN A NUTSHELL

In *The Third C: Check Out Your Data,* we discussed how to condense multiple individual values of a data item into a *summary value* for basic data review. Summary values are helpful in painting a general picture of the values of a numerical data item, instead of focusing on individual values. They are also known as *aggregates, aggregations, groupings,* or *summary statistics.* Examples include *sum, average, count, median, maximum,* and *minimum.* In this section, we demonstrate how to use the right summary value to solve real-world questions.

Sum versus average

To get the ball rolling, the regional sales managers want to know how their regions compare to the others.

Question: "What's the typical sale in each region?"

For each region, Maria **sums** all the sales transactions, and then graphs the total amount of sales.

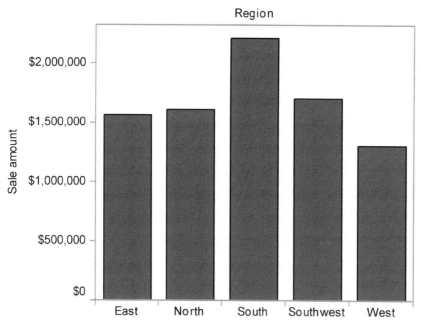

She realizes that the regions have different numbers of customers, so although the South has the highest total sales, she remembers that it also has the most customers.

Instead, she wants to see if the average sales transaction is different among the five regions. For this, she graphs the **average** sale amount instead of total sales.

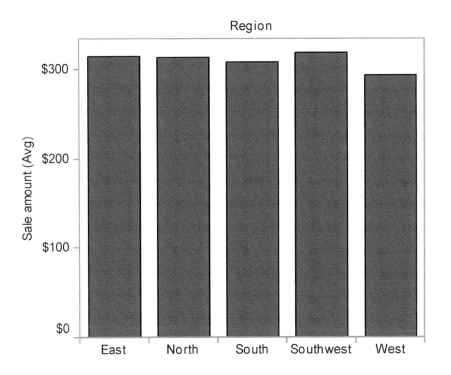

This is interesting—the average sale amount is similar in all five regions.

Take-Home Message

- Verify that you are using the appropriate summary value. One of the most common mistakes is to *sum* the data when it would be more useful to *average* the data.

Count versus count of unique occurrences

After some discussion about total and average sales by region, the sales managers are interested in following up on the anecdotal information that the South received the most orders.

Question: "How many orders were placed in each region?

Using the dataset of sales transactions, Maria charts the total number of sales transactions, or records, by region.

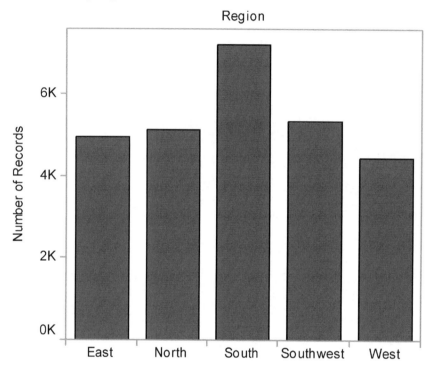

This is a **count** of the number of transactions. A single customer can be counted more than once if he or she made multiple purchases.

After examining this for a moment, she realizes that the managers really need the answer to a different question.

Question: "How many different customers ordered within each region?"

This is counting the number of **unique occurrences**, also called **count distinct**, of customers. In this case, the data item used was Customer ID, which is used to uniquely identify each customer.

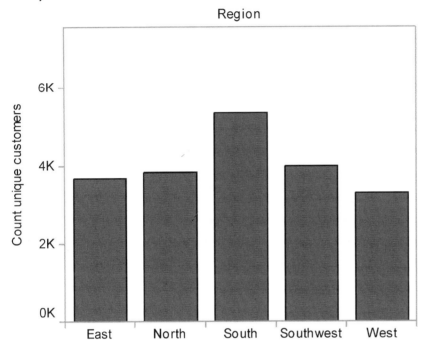

By using the count distinct data summary function, even customers who made multiple purchases are counted only one time. When you compare the two graphs, notice that the counts of unique customers are less than the counts of sales transactions.

Take-Home Message

- A common mistake is to *count* the number of records instead of *counting the number of unique or distinct items*, such as the distinct number of customers or products.

- Counts of unique occurrences are always equal to or less than counts of records from the same data.

- Often colleagues ask the wrong question, and it is your job to guide them to one that fits the problem.

Average versus median

Now the discussion turns to product lines sold by the company. One of the sales managers points out that Maria usually shows them charts of average sales by product line, but he is confused.

Question: "When I talk to salespeople, it seems that typical sale amounts are much lower than the averages. Why is this?"

Maria has an idea of what the problem may be. For comparison, she graphs **average** versus **median** sale amount for each product line.

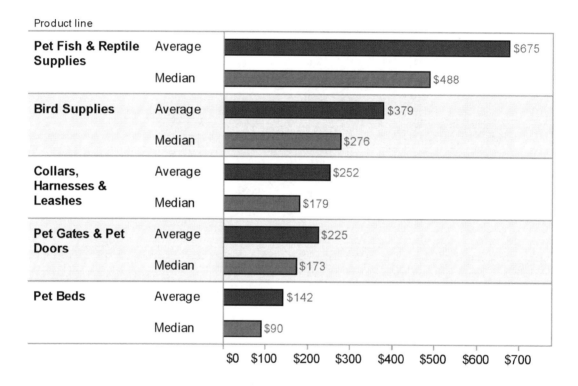

As we explained in detail in *The Third C: Check Out Your Data*, average is the sum of all the values for a data item, divided by the count of how many values are included in the average. The median is the data value or values right in the middle of your span of values for a particular numerical data item. In this particular dataset, the average sale is always higher than the median sale. To explain this, Maria uses a second chart, in which she plots each transaction.

Focus on the first product line, *Pet Fish & Reptile Supplies*, which has the largest difference between average ($675) and median ($488). Note that several transactions are very large. These are **outliers**, which "pull" the average higher. The median is a more accurate representation of the typical sale that is placed by customers.

Take-Home Message

- *Median* is often a more useful summary value than *average*, especially for data in which *outliers* can greatly alter the average value. However, people are very familiar with the idea of average, even though they often need the median value instead.

- Since average is the traditional summary value and people are used to it, it can be hard to convince both the analyst and the audience that the median may be more appropriate in certain cases.

- Typically, in business data, median is lower than average for positive metrics, such as sales. For negative metrics such as debt or spending, median is usually higher than average.

- There is a unique advantage to the average. If you are in a meeting and don't have access to your data analysis software, you can easily calculate the total or sum as long as you know the number of occurrences and the average.

Minimum and maximum versus percentiles

The sales managers would like to instruct the salespeople to follow up with customers that make large purchases, since they think there is a good chance that they will place large orders in the future.

Question: "For each product line, what should we consider a large purchase?"

Maria starts by displaying the **minimum** (or **min**) and **maximum** (or **max**) sale amount for each product line.

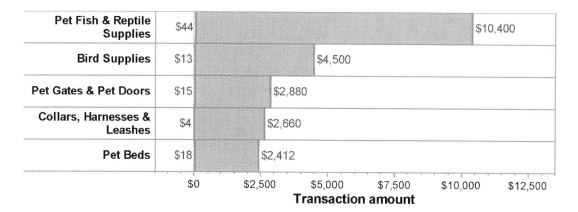

The gray area in between the two is the **span** or **range**. Similar to average, outliers also affect the min and the max.

To avoid this problem, Maria thinks that percentiles may be useful. She overlays the 5th and 95th percentiles on the range. It is interesting to remember that he min and max are the same as the 0th and 100th percentile!

5th and 95th percentiles overlaid on entire span of transactions for each product line

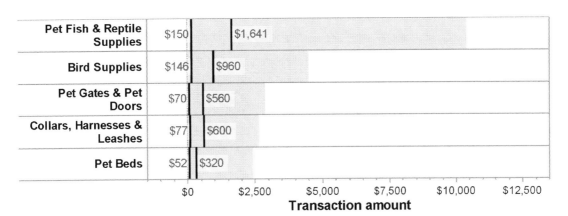

You may remember percentiles from your standardized testing days. The higher the percentile, the better you did. If you were in the 90th percentile, your score was in the top 10% of test-takers. Here, if a customer spent $1641 or more in *Pet Fish & Reptile Supplies*, he or she is in the 95th percentile of shoppers for that product line (which is uncommon). Spending $150 or less puts the customer in the 5th percentile, or bottom 5% of shoppers, and the bulk of the customers (90%) spent between $150 and $1641. Using percentiles essentially tells you what most of your customers did, and gets rid of unusual or typical transactions.

Maria also displays the 1st and 99th percentiles, to isolate the extreme values.

215

1st and 99th percentiles overlaid on entire span of transactions for each product line

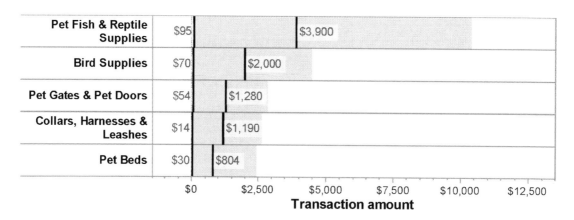

Look at *Pet Fish & Reptile Supplies*. The min is **$95**, compared to the min of **$44** when all the data are included. The max is **$3,900**, compared to the overall max of **$10,400**. So, removing only the top and bottom 1% drastically changes the min and the max.

Take-Home Message

- *Percentiles* can be more informative than *min* and *max*, and are useful if you are interested in describing most of your records for a data item, or the extreme top or bottom records.

- Use the 5th / 95th percentiles to capture common transactions.

- Use the 1st / 99th percentiles to eliminate extreme values.

- Percentiles can be a hard sell to businesspeople, as they are not commonly used. Once you illustrate how they are valuable, they will be more accepted.

TOPIC 2. SORT YOUR DATA: IDENTIFY THE MAJOR AND MINOR PLAYERS

This section builds upon the sorting basics that you learned in *The Third C: Check Out Your Data*. Sorting is not only a go-to technique, it also is powerful and flexible enough for more advanced analysis. If you would like your data listed or displayed in order of a particular data item, whether categorical or numerical, you can sort them to reorganize.

Order from highest to lowest: descending sort

Now the discussion turns to product popularity.

Question: "Which of our products were the most popular?"

Maria displays the count of unique customers that purchased each product.

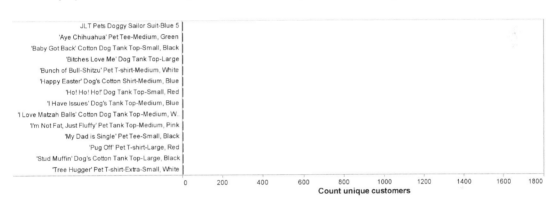

There are 652 products! The bars at the top of the chart are so tiny it is hard to see them, and there is a long scroll of products (not pictured here). Maria then sorts the products from the highest number of customers to the lowest number of customers, called **sorting in *descending* order of importance**, or **descending sort.**

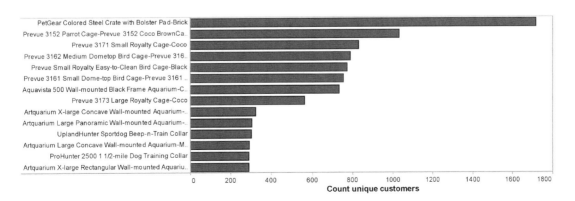

Now it is easy to see that relatively few of the products attracted a large number of customers. Though it is not shown in the screenshot, only the first 200 or so products are important.

Because Maria used the count of unique customers, a single customer is counted only once for a product, even if he or she purchased it more than once. Also, a single customer can buy multiple products, so he or she can be counted for each of those products.

Take-Home Message

- *Descending sort* is an extremely flexible and valuable tool for many business questions, especially if you have a long list of categories.

- If the question involves the words *best*, *most*, or *highest*, it's often a good way to start.

Order from lowest to highest: ascending sort

The sales managers are complaining that they have too many brand names of manufacturers to remember, and it seems to them that some don't sell well.

Question: "What are the lowest-selling brands?"

Maria displays the sales amount for each brand (not all brands are shown in the screenshot), and sorts in **ascending** order.

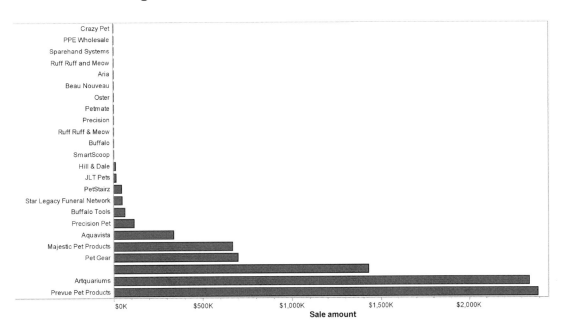

There are many brands that barely sell at all. Maybe they should be reviewed for possible elimination if similar-quality products are available from the bigger suppliers? This is useful information for the buyers.

Oops! There also are a few data quality issues, such as the brand Ruff Ruff and Meow being duplicated as Ruff Ruff & Meow, and one of the bars has no label at all.

Take-Home Message

- If the question involves the words *worst*, *least*, or *lowest*, *ascending sort* is a useful starting point.

- Always be on the lookout for data problems.

Sort within a sort: nested sort

The VP of sales is interested in information about their customer base.

Question: "Where are our customers located?"

Maria plans to show the VP how many customers are in each region, and then each state in the region. Maria does a **nested sort**, or **multi-sort**, in which a dataset is sorted by a data item, and then sorted again one or more times by additional data items, resulting in multiple tiers of sorted data items. Here, the metric being counted is the number of unique customers. The first tier of the sort divides the count of unique customers by region.

Unsorted count of unique customers by region

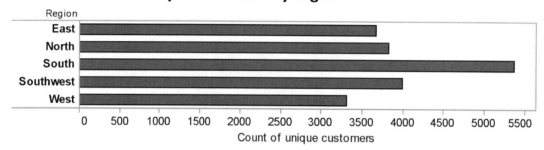

Descending sort, count of unique customers by region

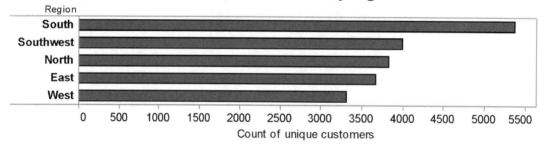

The second tier of the nested sort displays the count of unique customers, first by region and then by state.

Descending sort, count of unique customers by region, expanded by state (unsorted)

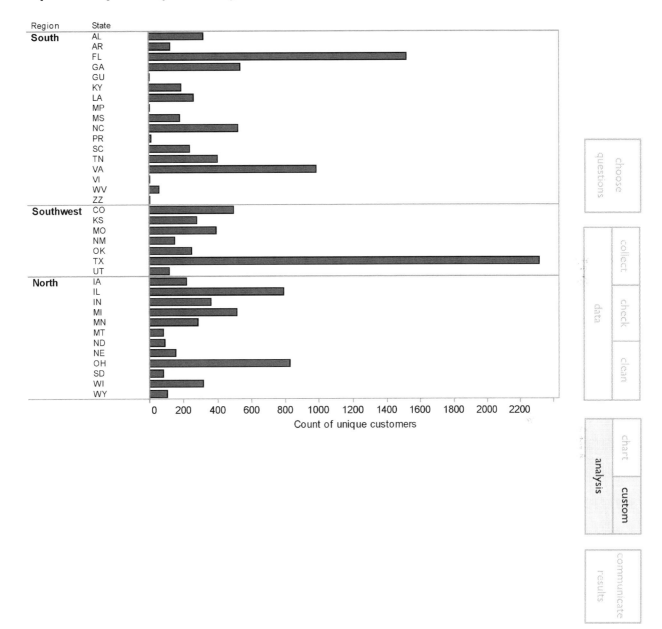

221

Nested descending sort with count of unique customers by region, then state

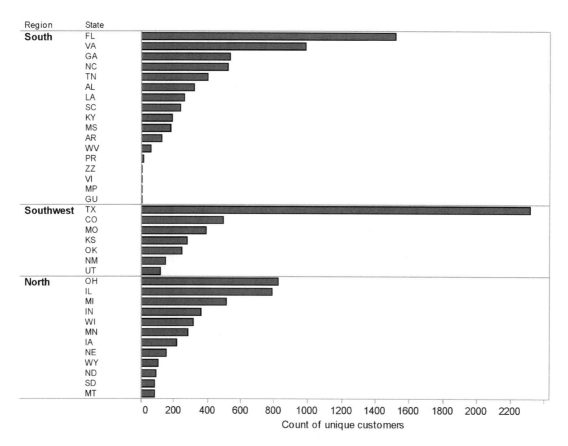

In the original descending sort, the VP can easily see that the South is the leader overall. In the nested descending sort, it is clear which states are important in each region, and that the Southwest has the best state for sales.

Take-Home Message

- If you have multiple levels of detail for a data item, such as location with region and state data, a *nested sort*, or *multi-sort*, may be useful.

- In a nested sort, a dataset is sorted by a data item, and then sorted again one or more times by additional data items, resulting in multiple tiers of sorted data items.

TOPIC 3. FILTER STARTER PACK:
UTILIZE THE POWER AND FLEXIBILITY OF FILTERS

We introduced basic filtering in *The Third C: Check Out Your Data*. Filters allow you to select or exclude particular values of either a categorical or numerical data item, such as a certain product, location, region, customer, date, or sales amount. Here we take you beyond basic data exploration to more advanced analysis using filters. Being adept at filtering is an invaluable tool for great analysts, but is often underrated as being less "glamorous" than other techniques.

Select particular categories

The sales managers observed that some customers have been requesting a larger selection of extravagant or luxury items, which the company has always thought of as a niche product line.

Question: "How many luxury products do we offer, and which ones have the highest sales?"

Maria filters to select the relevant categories, which are *Pet Jewelry* and *Pet Luxury* items. For comparison, she also selects *Pet Toys*, because the group knows more about that category and thinks that toys are very important to the customers. She plots the total sale amount for each product. She also sorts each category in descending order by sale amount.

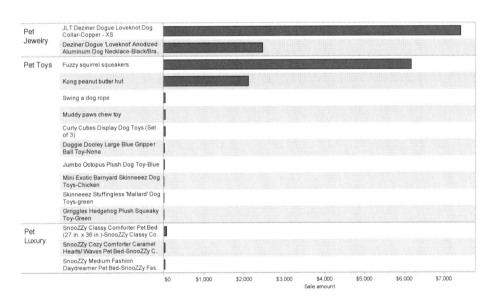

There are only two jewelry items, and they are the first and third best-selling items. This is surprising, since everyone guessed that toys would have sold much better than any of the extravagant items.

Also, there are three items in the *Pet Luxury* category, but for some reason, they're not doing well. Maybe the category needs to be featured or promoted, or replaced with more appealing products? Maria may want to share this preliminary finding with marketing, so they can figure out what needs to be changed.

Take-Home Message

- The most basic type of filter selects the categories or groups that you would like to focus on, while excluding unnecessary ones.

- Two tools can be better than one! In this example we filtered and then sorted to emphasize the top data items.

- An exciting aspect of doing analysis "on the fly" is that you often discover important information that you weren't looking for in the first place.

Search for "wildcards"

One of the managers notices a problem with the data.

Question: "Don't we sell more than two jewelry items?"

Maria does a **wildcard search** for the word "jewel".

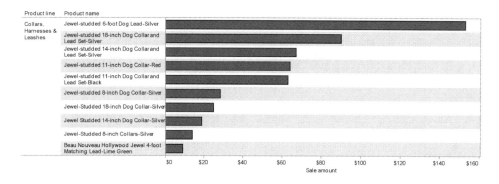

The sales manager was right; there are a lot more jewelry items—in a different category.

Take-Home Message

- As you may have discovered in your own job, data are rarely organized and categorized as widely expected.

- Sometimes you need to use your knowledge of the business to look for information in multiple ways.

Select individual records

The sales managers are interested in moving to a more general problem.

Question: "We'd like to know which products we should focus on to make big sales. Which product lines have the highest sale amounts?"

First, Maria graphs sale amount by product line for all transactions from the past two years and sorts in descending order.

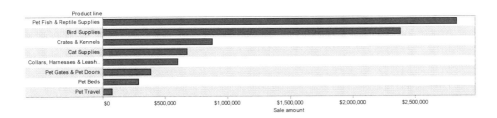

She focuses on the top eight product lines by sales, pictured here. *Pet Fish & Reptile Supplies* and *Bird Supplies* have the highest sales. However, it's hard to tell what percentage of the total sales amount comes from these two product lines. She changes the metric from sales amount to percent of the total sales amount.

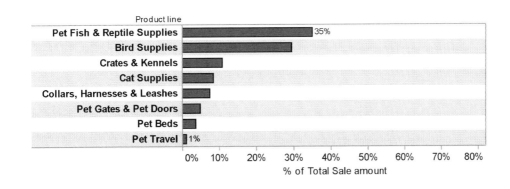

Now it is easier to see that *Pet Fish & Reptile Supplies* and *Bird Supplies* combined equal about two-thirds of total sales.

The sales managers are asking for information about which product lines result in big sales, so she realizes that she must filter to select large transactions. Since she is choosing **individual** transactions that fit the description, she is filtering at the record or row level, which is also referred to as the **lowest level of detail** because she can't choose anything smaller than a single transaction. This is different from filtering to select a particular category, as shown earlier. For instance, if she were to filter for purchases by product line, she would be selecting a group of transactions or records.

Using her knowledge of the business, she decides $1000 is the cutoff for a "big sale", so she filters to select all transactions that are more than $1000.

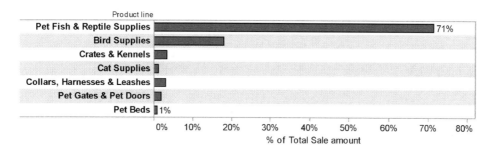

This is interesting. Together, *Pet Fish & Reptile Supplies* and *Bird Supplies* total more than 90% of the large sales. Note that *Pet Travel* is missing—this means that no transactions were greater than $1000.

Maria thinks that it may be useful to show the sales managers how the product lines change with smaller and smaller transaction amounts. She filters to select the transactions that are $1000 or less, down to amounts greater than $100.

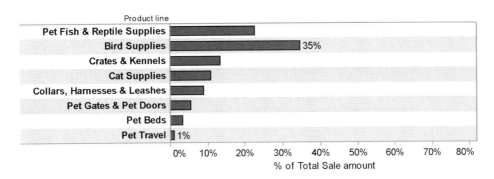

Although *Pet Fish & Reptile Supplies* and *Bird Supplies* are still more than half of the sales, they are not as dominant as in the large sales graph. Also, since *Pet Fish & Reptile Supplies* dropped to second place, there were probably only a few large transactions that made it number one for transactions greater than $1000.

Then Maria filters to select transactions $100 or less, down to greater than $50.

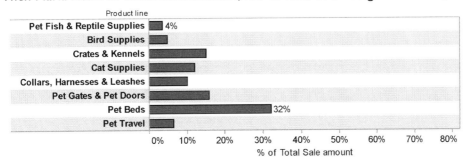

This totally changes the distribution of the sales by product line. *Pet Beds, Pet Gates & Pet Doors,* and *Crates & Kennels* are key lines in the lower transaction amounts.

In general, for successively smaller and smaller transaction amounts, the product lines further down the list become more important. So, by filtering at record level, Maria can see the differences regarding which product lines dominate at various price points.

Take-Home Message

- Filter at the individual record level if you are interested in the details of the data values, instead of the summary or aggregated values at the category level.

- Percent may be more useful than dollar amount if you would like to compare data filtered by different values in multiple views.

- It may be useful to break a metric into smaller groups such as $100-$999 or more than $1,000 to uncover detailed information.

- Take the initiative to show your colleagues something that they didn't directly ask, but may find useful to know.

FYI

We won't go into details here, but you may want to filter to select individual records by writing your own customized formulas that you develop for a specific problem.

This is also called filtering by **conditional values**. For instance, if you're interested in selecting customers who returned merchandise equal to more than 25% of their order amounts, you will need to write a specific formula for this purpose.

List the top or bottom performers

Since the company started by selling fish, bird, and reptile products, the sales managers are interested in how successful the expansion into dog and cat products has been.

Question: "How are sales in the dog and cat business?"

Maria thinks about the data items that she has available, and rewords the question so that she can analyze the data.

Maria's version of the question: "In which product line expansion categories are our best 200 customers spending the most money?"

She filters by category, retaining the dog and cat products, while excluding fish, bird, and reptile products. She then selects the top 200 customers, and graphs sale amounts by category, adding percent of the total sales for easy comparison. She also sorts in descending order, by sale amounts.

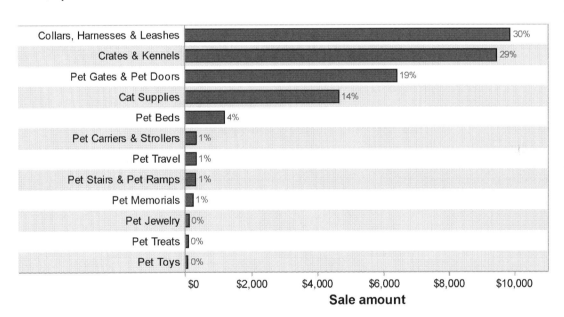

The majority of sales in expansion categories (95%) to the top customers were from the top five categories.

Take-Home Message

- Instead of including every category or record, it is often easier to focus on relevant subsets, commonly the top or bottom performers.

- Colleagues will sometimes ask you a general question, but you need to "translate" it into a more specific question that uses the data items that are available in your dataset. Try to paint a good picture of the requested information and possible limitations— Maria's choice was one of many possible questions.

- Filtering by the top or bottom performers is different from descending and ascending sorts, because you are selecting only a part of the dataset but often showing a different category of data than what you filtered by. In this example, we filtered to show the top 200 customers by sales, but graphed the expansion category product lines.

TOPIC 4. FILTERS TO SET THE DATES: FOCUS ON A PARTICULAR TIME PERIOD

Filters are incredibly flexible in selecting data for a time period of interest. Common analytical problems involve how results have changed over time or what has occurred in a given time span, so filters will be a crucial part of many of your analyses.

Specify individual dates

In May, the marketing department promoted different product lines on different days. On May 12, they promoted *Collars, Harnesses & Leashes*.

Question: "How were sales of collars, harnesses, and leashes on May 12?"

First, for context, Maria pulls up sales amount divided by product line for the entire month of May. She adds a label with the percentage that each product line contributed to the total sale amount (for instance, *Bird Supplies* was 29% of overall sales).

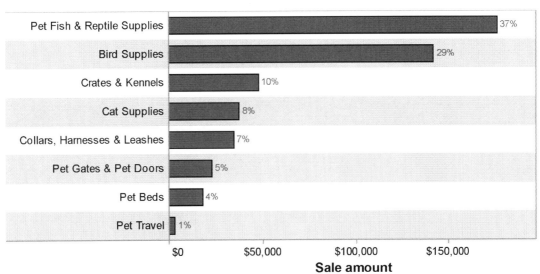

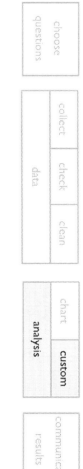

Then, she filters to select the individual date of May 12.

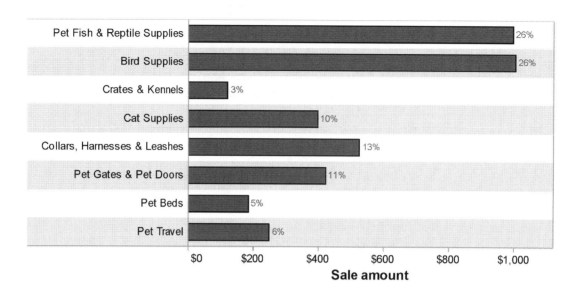

During the entire month, *Collars, Harnesses & Leashes* was 7% of the total sale amount. On May 12, this product line was 13%. Note that the scales are different between the two graphs, since Maria is comparing sales for a whole month to sales for one day. If she adjusted the scale for May 12 to the same one used for the entire month of May, the bars would be so tiny she wouldn't be able to read them. This is why the percentages are useful.

FYI

This is an example where statistical testing could be useful in determining if there was a truly meaningful increase in sales on May 12.

This is a relatively advanced topic, so if you are interested, consult a statistical reference.

Take-Home Message

- If someone requests to see what happened on a specific date, filtering is a quick and easy choice.

- It is extremely important that you provide the *relevant context* for comparison. Showing sales for only the day of a promotion isn't very useful if you don't know what sales normally are. Sales for the rest of the month or encompassing larger time periods indicate whether the promotion was successful or not.

- Use percentages to compare two graphs that have the same metrics, but very different scales.

FYI

Date offsets can be very useful when comparing two dates that you need to be similar, but differ in a relevant way.

For instance, you would like to compare sales on the 1st of the month for September and October. However, September 1st is a Thursday and October 1st is a Saturday, and sales are usually much higher on Thursday. You may want to use the first Thursday in October, October 6th, instead.

Define time periods

In 2010, the finance department complained that customers returning products for refunds were reducing profit margins. After extensive discussions with sales and the CEO, the company adjusted its return policies in 2011 to make it more difficult to return purchases.

Question: "In 2011, did returns decrease?"

Maria filters the dataset with all returns from 2010 and 2011 to select only the returns made in 2010. She also filters to retain the key product lines.

233

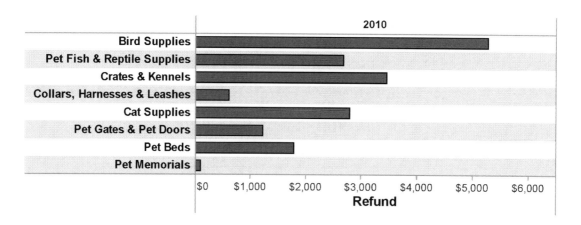

Maria then filters the original returns dataset to display only 2011. For accurate comparison, she ensures that the axes have the same scale, and labels the percent difference compared to 2010.

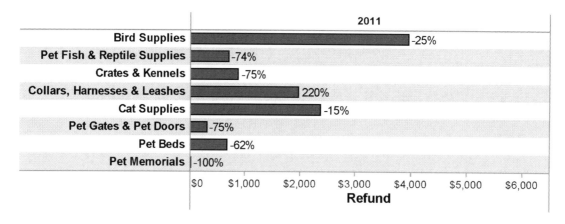

Great! Returns were down in almost every product line. For some reason, returns are up 220% in one product line, *Collars, Harnesses & Leashes*. Something appears to have gone wrong. If the data are correct, perhaps there is a problem with the quality of the products, so further analysis is required, perhaps by investigating manufacturers or products.

Maria could have condensed the information with a multi-pane bar chart.

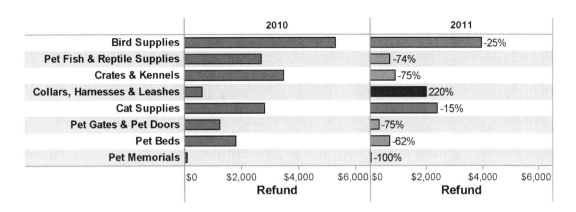

The darker the bar in the 2011 pane, the higher the growth in refunds in 2011 compared to 2010.

Take-Home Message

- Choosing certain time periods can help you easily compare what happened in one time period with another. Filtering for defined time periods can be useful to just get a sense of what is going on with metrics of interest. However, it is also useful to see how the business was affected by actions that your company took or events that happened in the outside world.

- Filtering your data repeatedly allows you to rapidly examine very specific data.

- You will frequently encounter strange results in your analysis that might require further investigation. It may be as simple as you making a mistake in specifying the question, pulling the data, or performing the analysis, or there may be something wrong with the dataset. Finally, it may be the reality that was unexpected.

Adjust date ranges

The VP of sales is interested in evaluating the 2011 holiday sales season. Additionally, to attract more of the dog and cat market, he had instructed the sales managers to heavily promote collars and leashes.

Question: "How were sales during the 2011 holiday season? Did collar and leash sales increase?"

First, Maria realizes that she must display two holiday seasons to make a useful comparison. She decides that the holiday season starts the day after Thanksgiving (Black Friday) and ends on Christmas Day (to include the last-minute shoppers). Black Friday was on November 25 in 2010 and November 24 in 2011, and Christmas is always on December 25.

For 2010, she filtered to select the range of November 25 to December 25.

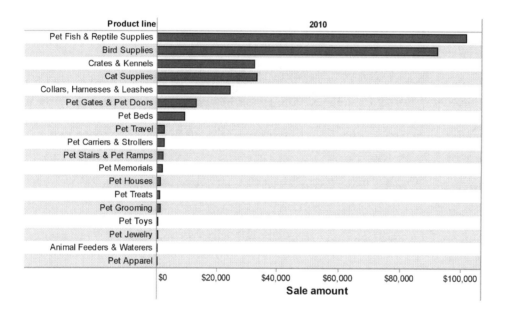

Then, for 2011, she filtered to choose the range of November 24 to December 25.

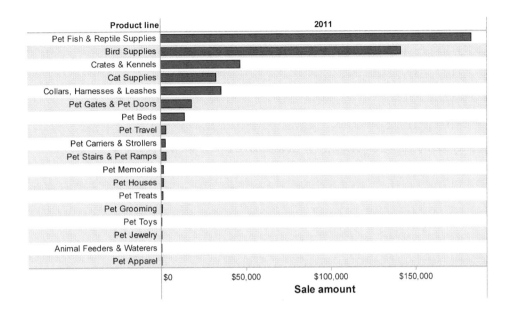

This is confusing, because the scales for 2010 and 2011 are different, so it isn't clear how sales changed in 2011. Maria adjusts the scale for 2010 to be the same as 2011.

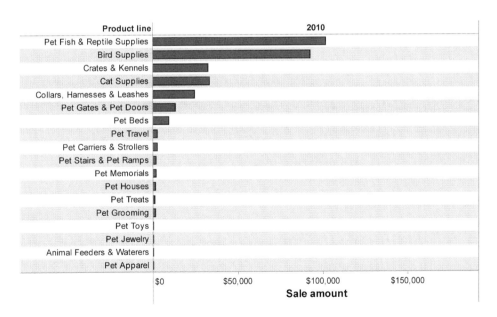

Great news! Overall, sales were up in the 2011 holiday season. *Collars, Harnesses & Leashes* overtook *Cat Supplies*. Although most of the product lines were up, *Cat Supplies* was flat. Maria made a note to herself to update marketing about *Cat Supplies*.

Heads Up

Use the simplest chart that will answer your question.

For instance, perhaps you thought line charts would work better here. First of all, since there are many product lines, there would be many lines on one graph. Second, since the team is interested in the entire time period between Black Friday and Christmas, not what happened day-by-day, there's no need to show the detailed daily data. Third, the full mix of product lines can easily be compared in the bar chart, to see which ones are important and which ones aren't.

Additionally, you could simplify comparisons between the years by using a multi-pane bar chart.

Take-Home Message

- Filtering to adjust the date range is a useful way to pull up a specific subset of data.

- If you're interested in the entire data range, not in specific days, weeks, etc., for simplicity show only the full range and not the details.

- In analysis, it is not uncommon to be investigating one issue only to also find a different, unexpected one.

FYI

Relative dates may be useful in certain situations.

Use relative dates to confine the display of your metric to a consistent and prior time interval that is relative to the current date. Specify the metric and the number of recent years, quarters, months, weeks, or days, such *as sales in the past five quarters* or *number of customer service calls in the past seven days.*

TOPIC 5. CASCADING FILTERS:
CHOOSE SPECIFIC DATA WITH A SERIES OF FILTERS

By this point, you may have had enough of different filters. However, in this section, you get a break, because we are simply combining filter types that you've already seen. You can mix and match filter types in a sequence of **cascading filters**, a network or series of interconnected filters that allow you to quickly choose highly specific data. This is useful for answering rapid-fire questions "on the fly".

The managers ask if they can take a half-hour to look at sale amounts for various locations, customers, and product information.

Question: "Can we see sales for each product line?"

Maria graphs all the sales data by product line, and adds filters for region, state, zip code, and customer name.

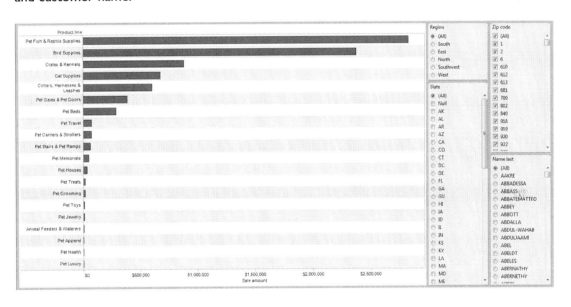

239

Question: "What about sales in the West only?"

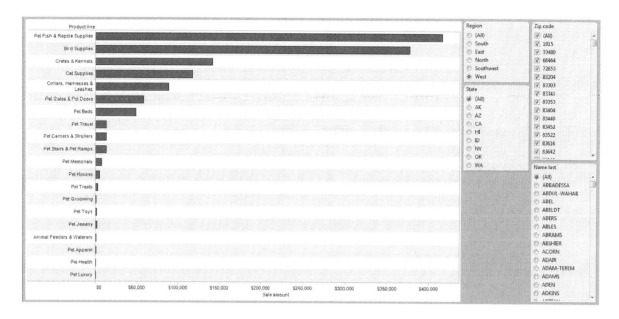

Question: "Can you pull up the state of Washington, and select only products that have warranties of 90 days or less from all manufacturers?"

Maria adds filters for warranty type and manufacturer.

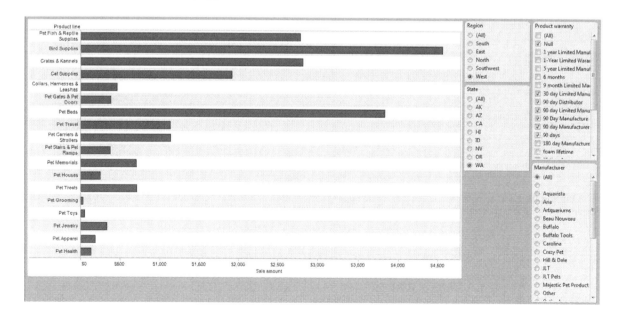

Question: "Can we see only the items from Majestic Pet Products that have no warranty?"

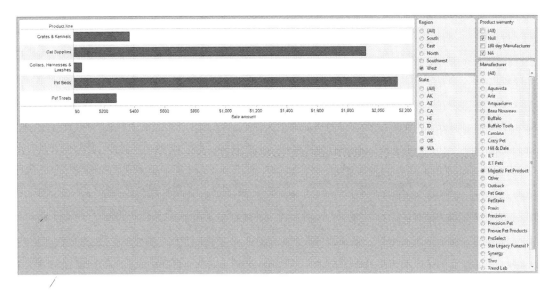

Take-Home Message

- *Cascading filters* are a great time-saver, as they allow you to quickly pull up specific subsets of data.

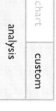

TOPIC 6. RIGHT METRIC FOR THE JOB: EXPRESS METRICS IN THE MOST INFORMATIVE WAY

Sometimes it's not what you say, but how you say it! Often you can answer difficult questions by simply re-stating your data items in a different way. In this section, we explain a variety of techniques to get the most information out of your metrics by re-expressing them as new metrics that help you address the problem at hand.

Rank important metrics for easy identification

The VP of sales is thinking about combining the West and the Southwest into one region.

Question: "What are the best states in the combined West and Southwest regions?"

Since the question involves locations (in this case, states), Maria uses a map. Rather than clutter the map by labeling the sales amounts, she ranks the states by total sales over the past two years.

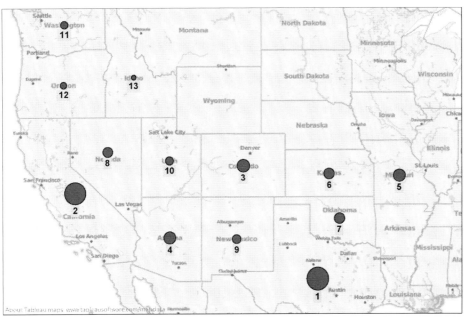

Sale amount

○	$3,959
	$200,000
	$400,000
	$600,000
	$800,000
	$1,011,011

The size of the bubble represents the total sales amounts for last two years (the bigger the bubble, the higher the sales). In total sales, Texas is first and California is second. If anyone is interested in the actual sales numbers, Maria includes the legend.

Take-Home Message

- *Ranking* can be useful if the order from highest to lowest is more important than the exact values, as it is quick and easy to understand.

- If a question involves *locations*, a map is often a great place to start.

Incorporate external data sources

The VP of sales points out that Texas and California are very large states.

Question: "Can you adjust the rankings based on how many people live in the state?"

Maria is able to find state population data on the U.S. census website. She calculates average sales amount per 1,000 residents and puts the rankings on a map.

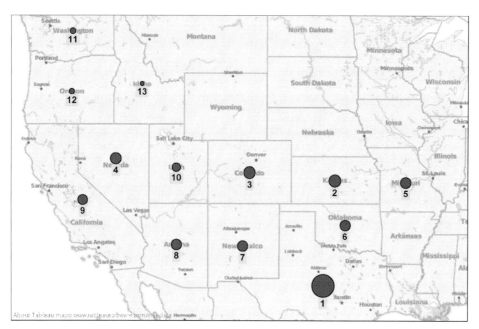

Sale amount per thousand residents

$3
$50
$100
$150
$215

While Texas remains first, Kansas is now second, and California is ninth. The sales VP concludes that, assuming sales in California could reach the same high level as in Texas, there is a lot of room for growth in the California market, as it has not been fully "penetrated" (a marketing and sales term).

Take-Home Message

- You may be able to quickly increase the relevance and value of your analysis by incorporating data from external sources.

FYI
The term *per capita* is often used when analyzing population data.
It means the average per person, or "for each head".

Compare the leader to the pack

As part of planning the marketing budget by state, the marketing department requested sales information from the VP of sales.

Question: "The New Jersey sales manager is requesting the same advertising budget as in Texas. Based only on sales, is that reasonable?"

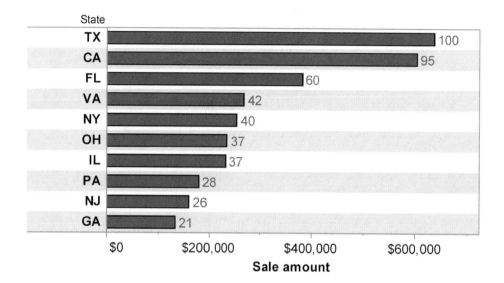

The numbers next to the bars are an **index**: Texas is number one in sales, so it has an index value or number of 100. The index numbers for the other states are all relative to Texas, so Maria can quickly compare them to the leader, with only simple calculations. Maria points out that sales in New Jersey (index number = 26) are only a quarter of sales in Texas (100), which was determined by dividing 26 by 100 (26%). Unless there is the possibility that sales will explode (for instance, a major competitor went bankrupt in New Jersey), the request to spend as much advertising money as in Texas is likely unreasonable.

> ## FYI
>
> An introduction to calculating index numbers is in the FYI box under the *Time Travel Scenario (#4)*, in *The Fifth C: Chart Your Analysis.*
>
> If you decide to use index numbers, consult a statistical manual.

Take-Home Message

- Often people know a lot about the leader in a category or metric, so making comparisons to the leader gives them a useful point of reference.

247

Percentage of the overall total or average

The sales managers have follow-up questions about the expansion product lines of dog and cat products that were discussed earlier in the meeting.

Question: "Can you give us pie charts that show if the important expansion product lines got better or worse from 2010 to 2011?"

Maria creates two pie charts of sales amount—one for 2010 and one for 2011. She includes the top seven product lines (including *Pet Fish & Reptile Supplies* and *Bird Supplies* for comparison).

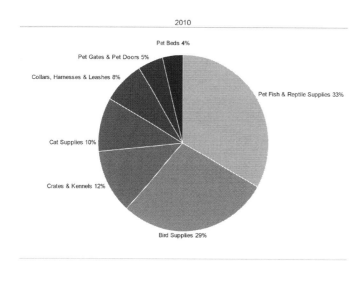

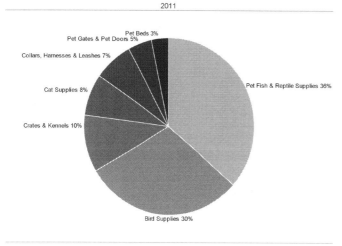

Each pie slice is labeled with the percentage of the product line's sales that contributes to all sales for that year, called *percentage of the total, percentage-to-whole, part-to-whole,* or *ratio.* The sales managers have to study both the pie charts to compare the product lines between the two years.

Instead, Maria converts the two pie charts to a multi-pane bar chart.

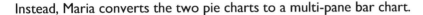
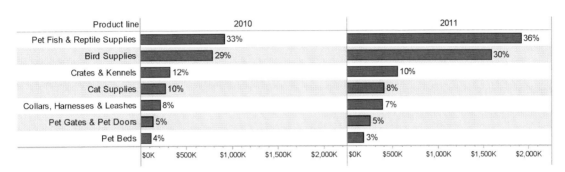

Each bar is labeled with percent contribution to total sales for the year, and dollar amounts are added on the horizontal axis. Now, the managers can quickly see the differences in the expansion product lines (the 3rd through the 7th product lines down the list) between the two years, as well as sales in dollars if necessary. Sales in all the product lines stayed the same or decreased *as a percent of overall sales that year.* They also can see that the first two product lines increased their share of overall sales in 2011.

Take-Home Message

- *Percentage of the total* is useful to determine the contribution of a particular category to the total amount, and how contributions changed over time.

- If colleagues ask for pie charts, also show them a bar chart with the same information.

Year-to-date (YTD) total

The sales managers are wondering how business is in the current year for their regions.

Question: "How are sales doing this year in each region?"

Maria calculates the **year-to-date totals (YTD)**. Since it is 22 days into the current year, Maria also graphs the first 22 days of last year for comparison.

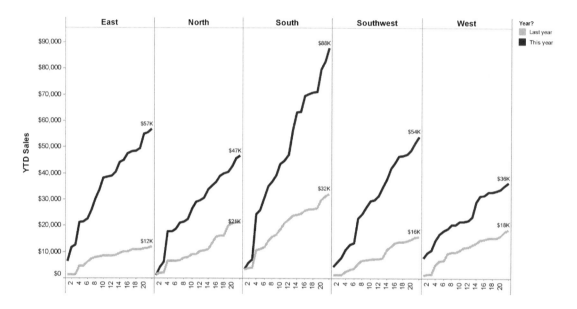

Good news—in all 5 regions, sales are up this year compared to last. Additionally, sales have been *increasing at a greater rate* as the year progresses, as shown by the *increasing distances between the lines* for the two years.

Take-Home Message

- To paint a more complete picture when comparing overall performance this year to last, *year-to-date* or *cumulative totals* should be compared to similar time periods from previous years.

Year-over-year (YOY) growth rate

The sales VP has a printed page from marketing with the promotional spending by month and product line for 2010 and 2011. He would like to compare sales to the promotions.

Question: "Which months and product lines did better this year than last?"

Maria thinks that **year-over-year (YOY) growth rate** in sales would be a simple yet useful way to answer this question. YOY growth rate compares a metric, such as sales, in one year to the same metric in the previous year to determine how much the metric increased or decreased between the two years. She graphs total sales amounts for both years, subdivided by quarter into panes for easy comparison.

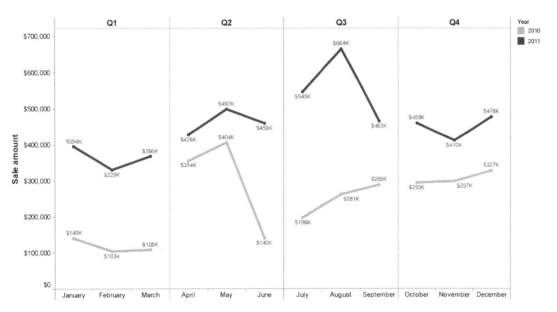

It's easy to see that for all quarters in 2011, sales were much higher compared to 2010. However, labeling dollar amounts on the chart makes it difficult to see how much higher. Maria replaces the dollars with percent growth, commonly referred to as growth rate.

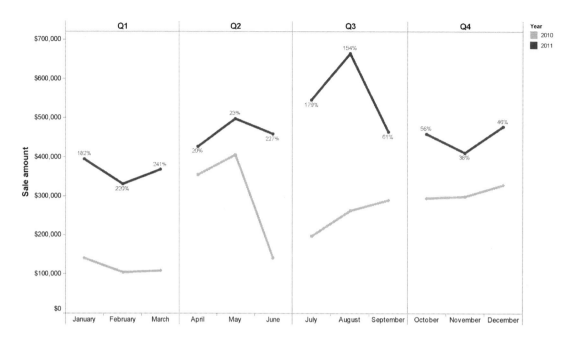

The growth rate is highly variable, ranging from a min of 20% (April) to a max of 227% (June). So, sales were up 20% YOY in April, and 227% YOY in June. The sales managers ask Maria to break this chart down by product line across the year. Once Maria graphs this, she sorts the product lines from highest to lowest, and labels the 2011 bars with growth rate.

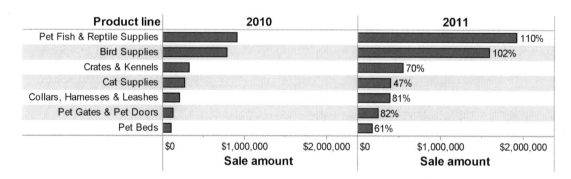

YOY growth rates range from a min of 47% for *Cat Supplies* to a max of 110% for *Pet Fish & Reptile Supplies*.

Take-Home Message

- *Year-over-year (YOY) growth rate* simplifies the comparison of two years by summarizing the changes between them, instead of comparing the ratios of two dollar values repeatedly.

- Comparisons can be made at multiple times throughout the year, depending on the frequency of the data (quarter, month, etc.) For example, you could compare the sales in Q2 of 2011 with Q2 of 2010 or the sales of May 2011 with May 2010.

- YOY growth eliminates the *baseline effect*—in a graph, growth starting at a smaller value appears to be less than equal growth starting at a higher value. To illustrate, 50% growth for a baseline of $1,000 is an additional $500. For a baseline of $100,000, 50% growth is an additional $50,000. The second example dwarfs the first, so people assume growth is much higher.

- You also can compare quarter-over-quarter growth rates, month-over-month, etc.

choose questions

collect data | check | clean

analysis | chart | **custom**

communicate results

TOPIC 7. RELATIONSHIPS: OBSERVE HOW ONE DATA ITEM CHANGES WITH ANOTHER

In this section we explain various types of relationships between data items, including categorical relationships and correlations.

Categorical relationships: ordinal and nominal

Helpful Hint
We previously used the term categorical when describing data item in *The Second C.* This topic describes the different types of relationships that can exist within categorical data items.

Since the finance department is quite concerned about return rates, the VP follows up on this topic. Although it is counterintuitive, people will often hold on to products with lifetime warranties, even if they have small problems with them, since they know it is possible to request repairs in the future.

Question: "If we sell more products with lifetime warranties, will it decrease the return rate?"

Maria recently performed a *customer segmentation analysis*, in which she divided customers into four groups based on their purchases and demographic information. She incorporates the *customer segments* into her analysis, displaying warranty terms and return rates for each segment.

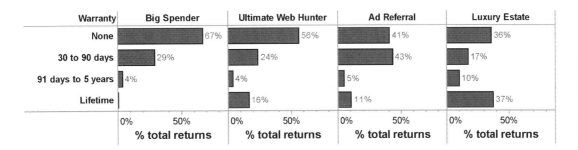

Warranty is divided into four groups: *None, 30 to 90 days, 91 days to 5 years*, and *Lifetime*. These groups relate to each other in a particular order, as *None* is a shorter time period than *30 to 90 days*, which in turn is shorter than *91 days to 5 years*, which is shorter than *Lifetime*. If you listed these groups in a different order, it would be confusing. Warranty is an **ordinal** category, because the groups must be listed in a specific order to be meaningful (ordinal and order derive from the same root, "ordo", which means "series"). Note that each group contains a different time period—*30 to 90 days* is based on a number of days, *91 days to 5 years* is based on days and years, and *None* and *Lifetime* contain no time period.

The four groups of customer segments do not relate to each other in a particular way, at least in the sense that they can be ordered from lowest to highest, shortest to longest, fastest to slowest, etc. (unless you order them based on a specific metric). Customer segment is a **nominal** category, because the segments can be listed in any order, as the relationship of one to another is not dependent on the order of the list (nominal means "in name only"). Although nominal categories are often listed alphabetically, this is simply an order based on the label—this order has no real meaning when analyzing the data.

Returning to the question, Maria notices that all four segments behave very differently. Perhaps what stands out most is that *Luxury Estate* has the highest return rate for products with lifetime warranties, which is different from the other segments; perhaps they are the *least* concerned about warranties. Maria makes a note to investigate this further.

Categorical relationships: interval

The sales managers would like more information on repeat customers.

Question: "Do repeat customers spend more if they shop more?"

Maria graphs the sale amount versus the number of distinct transactions (from 1 to 8 on the horizontal axis). The circles are customers and the horizontal black lines are average sale amounts. She adds the 5th and 95th percentiles, which bound the gray areas.

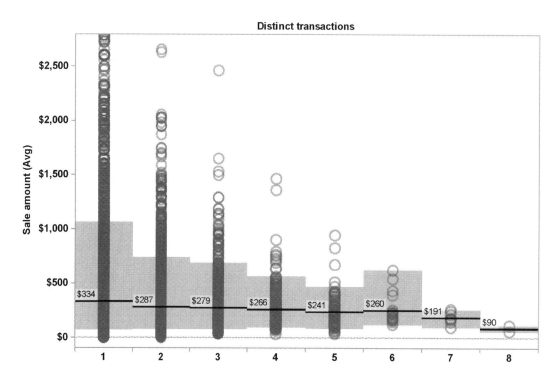

The transactions are divided into eight groups, **1 through 8**. They are listed in a logical order that would not make sense if rearranged, similar to an ordinal category. Additionally, there is a known and equal size difference between the groups. Each group has customers who made one more transaction than those in the previous group, and if more groups were to be included, you could easily guess that they would be **9** transactions, **10** transactions, etc. This is an **interval** category. The ordinal category of warranty shown in the previous example would be an interval if the groups were *1 to 30 days, 31 to 60 days, 61 to 90 days,* and *91 to 120 days.*

Maria notices that in general, the average sales amount decreases with each additional transaction. However, as the number of transactions increases, there are fewer customers, so generalizing from the data becomes less and less reliable, especially at **7** and **8**.

Take-Home Message

- **Types of categorical relationships**

  - *Nominal* = order not important

  - *Ordinal* = order important, irregular group sizes

  - *Interval* = order important, regular group sizes

Correlations

The sales team is curious if they are making a profit on every sale, or if some of their sales are "bad".

Question: "How much of our profit per transaction is based on the sale amount?

Since this question is asking how a particular outcome, profit, is affected by the value that most likely influences it, sales, Maria realizes that analyzing the **correlation** between the two would be useful.

She uses a scatter plot to graph *profit* on the vertical axis and *sales* on the horizontal axis. Each circle represents a single sale of a particular product. So, one product can be represented by many circles.

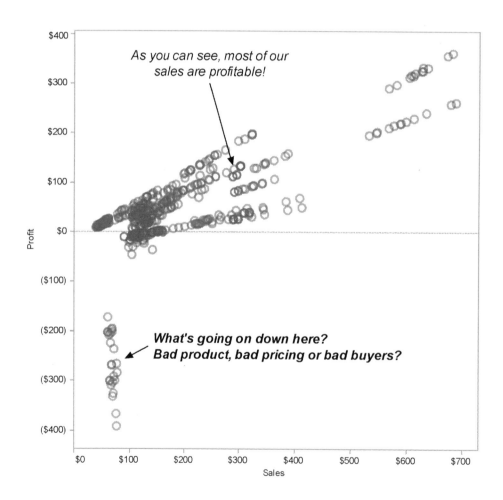

This is a "profit versus sales" graph, one of the most common applications of correlation analysis. Based on her knowledge of the business, Maria concludes that as sales increase, profit usually increases, but not always. She also makes a note to further investigate why there is negative profit in quite a few of the low dollar sales.

Take-Home Message

- *Correlation* is the tendency of one measure to change based upon how another measure changes.

- Simply because two metrics are correlated does not mean that one "causes" the other. You may know enough about your business and the metrics that you have a pretty strong feeling about one causing the other.

- **Caution**: If you are making an expensive or critical decision, first look into the assumptions and limitations of correlation analysis. There are many books and articles on the topic.

Heads Up
After working through this C, feel free to return to earlier C's. For instance, you may have pulled the wrong data. Just don't skip important steps along the way, such as checking out and cleaning up the new data.

RECAP OF THE SIXTH C: CUSTOMIZE YOUR ANALYSIS

A pessimist sees the difficulty in every opportunity;
an optimist sees the opportunity in every difficulty.

—WINSTON CHURCHILL
British prime minister
influential in politics for over five decades and
recipient of the Nobel Prize in Literature

Topic 1. Summary values

Describe your data items in a nutshell
- Sum versus average
- Count versus count of unique occurrences
- Average versus median
- Minimum and maximum versus percentiles

Topic 2. Sort your data

Identify the major and minor players
- Order from highest to lowest: descending sort
- Order from lowest to highest: ascending sort
  - Sort within a sort: nested sort

Topic 3. Filter starter pack

Utilize the power and flexibility of filters
- Select particular categories
- Search for "wildcards"
- Select individual records
  - *FYI box*: Conditional values
- List the top or bottom performers

Topic 4. Filters to set the dates

Focus on a particular time period
- Specify individual dates
  - *FYI box*: date offsets
- Define time periods
- Adjust date ranges
- *FYI box*: relative date

Topic 5. Cascading Filters

Choose specific data with a series of filters

Topic 6. Right metric for the job

Express metrics in the most informative way
- Rank important metrics for easy identification
- Incorporate external data sources
- Compare the leader to the pack
- Percentage of the overall total or average
- Year-to-date (YTD) total
- Year-over-year (YOY) growth rate

Topic 7. Relationships

Observe how one data item changes with another
- Categorical relationships: ordinal and nominal
- Categorical relationships: interval
- Correlations

Congratulations! You've made it through the hard part. Don't worry if you can't remember everything, because you can always refer back for details.

All you have left is pulling the first six C's together to present what you found to your colleagues, so that they can take action. Move on to *The Seventh C: Communicate Your Results.*

Visit **http://www.AccidentalAnalyst.com** *to sign up for our newsletter with information about upcoming live training, webinars, tips, books and more!*

THE SEVENTH C: COMMUNICATE YOUR RESULTS

You can have brilliant ideas,
but if you can't get them across,
your ideas won't get you anywhere.

—LEE IACOCCA
Engineer, member of the original Ford Mustang design team,
and CEO during Chrysler's comeback in the 1980's

Unless the analysis is for your eyes only, you have one more step after you finish analyzing your business questions. It's time to effectively communicate your results—including insights and decisions—to your boss, colleagues, or clients. Pulling all the C's together to communicate your results is the finale of your analysis. If you present your findings well, your audience will understand the value of the analysis, because you've pointed out a better way for the company or department to attain its goals. It's like walking down the red carpet!

Slide shows, discussions during group meetings, e-mails, memos, or written reports are all formats that you can use to present results. No matter which format you use, it is important to clearly state the questions you selected, what you found, and your decisions or recommendations to the decision-makers. An added bonus is that the time spent preparing your presentation is a great opportunity to review your work so you can remind yourself of what you did, look for mistakes, and organize the content.

Heads Up

In this C, we focus on assessing how well you communicate the results of your analysis, rather than on general presentation skills.

Most of you have probably put together some type of presentation. Additionally, there are entire books focused on helping you with presentation skills (see the *Further Reading* list at the end of the book).

Similar to *The First C: Choose Your Questions*, successful communication is a combination of art and science. It is essential to evaluate how effectively your deliverable or final work product explains the importance of the analysis to your audience. In *The Seventh C: Communicate Your Results*, we've developed a checklist of benchmarks, useful as a framework for both creating your presentation **and** assessing its quality.

ARE YOU A STRAIGHT "A" COMMUNICATOR? THESE BENCHMARKS WILL HELP YOU "GRADE" YOURSELF.

Does your slide deck or report contain...

Audience-appropriate results?

Answers to the right questions?

Applicable metrics?

Attractive visuals?

Actionable insights, recommendations, and decisions?

Attention-grabbing storylines?

In this C, we describe each benchmark and ways to verify that you've done a good job of incorporating it into the presentation. At the end of each description, we demonstrate how to apply it using a case study of the pet supply company,

Helpful Hint
By this point, you may be thinking "I've learned all these C's, and now there's a list of A's?" There's no need to remember this list—it's arranged by A's so that when you are in a rush to prepare a presentation, it's easy to run through the benchmarks to ensure that you've addressed all of them.

In *The Sixth C: Customize Your Analysis*, Maria the analyst led a series of interactive meetings with the VP of sales and the regional sales managers, answering a wide variety of questions on the spot about the company's sales data. Overall, the company had a phenomenal year. The marketing managers heard about the exciting news and would like to know the best path forward to continue the company's success into the future. In particular, they are interested in knowing *which states in the U.S. have the best growth potential for sales expansion.*

To address this issue, Maria is preparing a short slide presentation and organizing her content using the benchmarks.

Helpful Hint

To see illustrations of the information in this C, you can download Maria's sample slide show in color at www.AccidentalAnalyst.com.

choose questions

collect data | check | clean

chart | custom | analysis

communicate results

AUDIENCE-APPROPRIATE RESULTS

Information is a source of learning.
But unless it is organized, processed, and available
to the right people in a format for decision making,
it is a burden, not a benefit.

—C. WILLIAM POLLARD
former CEO of ServiceMaster, Fortune 500
company that owns Merry Maids and Terminix

We've all attended talks or read reports that offer an excessive amount of details, many of which were irrelevant to the current issue or just plain overwhelming. Unfortunately, the presenter may have had a great story to tell, but it was buried in too much information for the audience to become interested or follow the main points.

Make it easy for people to listen to
or read your story!

If you remember only one point from this C, this is it. When you are preparing any type of presentation, keep in mind that since you are telling a story, the best way to engage your audience is to provide only the relevant details. It's easy to think, "I just want them to understand all of my hard work" or "I want them to see all the details of how I reached my conclusion"—but if you include too much information, you're hiding both the value of your analysis and possibly how well you know the data. Keep the story brief and frame it in terms that will inform and hopefully excite the audience.

Find out:

Which departments are involved and how are they evaluated for success?

Different departments have different goals, so adjust the information depending upon whether it's Sales, Finance, Marketing, IT, etc. For instance, IT may appreciate the details, while salespeople want a simple plan that they can immediately put into action.

What are the jobs and levels of the team?

Think about what level of detail these people will care about. Upper management typically has less time for details, but as you move down the chain, more detail may be needed to implement the plan.

Is the nature of the decision strategic, operational or analytical?

These terms were described in *The First C: Choose Your Questions*, but here's a brief synopsis:

- *Strategic* analyses are developed for executives, middle management, or business owners. These analyses help them make decisions that will probably affect long-term priorities for the business. They typically prefer fewer details and simple, clear presentation of results relative to stated company goals.

- *Operational* analyses are for teams monitoring live systems, such as overall data center performance or how well a call center is handling customer issues. These analyses usually require a summary of performance over the past few days or hours relative to expectations.

- *Analytical* analyses are for analysts investigating key issues and potential actions. These range from high-level summaries to very detailed reviews "below the covers" to explore possible causes of problems. These can be quite complex, walking through the steps of most of the analysis. Your fellow analysts may be able to offer additional ideas or data to enhance your work.

What is the environment where the presentation will be delivered?

If it's a busy, hectic meeting where people have only a few minutes, think of how you'd feel sitting there with a long, detailed slide show. You wouldn't have time to absorb the information! It would be better to use the limited time to share your key findings, and let the audience know you have additional information for those who are interested. On the other hand, if the members of your audience want to use a written report to plan strategy for the next year, they have more time to work through detailed information, so a thorough report may be useful.

As you work through the rest of this C, keep your presentation on track by focusing on your target audience. Use clear examples that demonstrate key results and insights, verifying that your colleagues will relate to them by putting yourself in their shoes.

Case Study: Audience

Maria's audience for her slide presentation is mid-level marketing managers. Since they are looking at a long-term plan to determine in which states to focus marketing spending, based on the best growth potential, this is a **strategic problem**. So, her goal is a simple, clear analysis, explained in terms marketers will understand, with some, but not every, detail.

She makes a note to explain her analysis by including only the key steps that the audience can understand, with easy-to-read, simple charts.

ANSWERS TO THE RIGHT QUESTIONS

*There's no sense in being precise
when you don't even know what you're talking about.*

—JOHN VON NEUMANN
Hungarian-American mathematician
who made major contributions to economics, statistics, nuclear weaponry,
computer science, and quantum mechanics, among other fields

The foundation of your story is built upon the questions that were the point of your analysis. To verify that you stayed on track, ask yourself:

Did I effectively answer my questions?

It is quite common for analysts to obtain what appear to be useful results, including very interesting ones, but upon closer inspection they realize they failed to answer the relevant questions.

Are they the right questions?

These are the ones the target audience cares about. Revisit the typical points of reference and cues that helped you to translate the problem at hand into useful questions at the start of the analysis.

To assess the quality of your questions, refer to *The First C: Choose Your Questions*, in which we covered this topic in detail.

Once you are confident that you have answers to the right questions, developing the core of your presentation should be simple—*state the questions you asked and the answers that you found*. Use only terms that your audience can understand.

Case Study: Answers

Maria understood the overall issue that the marketing team was interested in—finding which states have the best growth potential for sales. To find out how they're going to take action with the results, she spoke with one of the marketing managers. He told her that they're planning a flyer campaign, which will be direct-mailed or placed in newspapers. While they could distribute them around the entire country, past experience has taught them that spreading the message thinly across many states works poorly. Instead, they decided that the money will be much more effective if they repeatedly market in a few states, creating a strong image to allow them to compete with much larger pet companies.

Great! Now she knows the question they need answered:

> *"Which states are worth spending marketing money in during the upcoming flyer campaign, based upon the best sales growth potential?"*

APPLICABLE METRICS

The best measure of a man's honesty
isn't his income tax return.
It's the zero adjust on his bathroom scale.

—ARTHUR C. CLARKE
Author of *2001: A Space Odyssey*

To tell your story, use the *best metrics available to answer the question of interest*, assuming they meet the following criteria:

- Simplest metrics that make your point

- Relevant to audience

- Not too technical for audience

- Data are accessible to you

If you are introducing a new metric to your audience because no other metric is appropriate, it is helpful to start with a familiar metric for context before introducing the better, more relevant one.

Here are some examples of important variations of similar metrics:

- *gross sales* versus *net sales?*

- *counts* versus *percents?*

- *sales per state* versus *sales per capita per state?*

- *time to ship* versus *time to ship compared to target* versus *time to ship compared to historical norms?*

Case Study: Applicable metrics

Using her knowledge of both the company and available data, Maria listed the most useful metrics for the marketing department's goals of finding the best states for potential growth.

The marketing managers told her they were looking at *total sales per state* and *total sales per customer per state.*

Maria thought this was a good starting point, and came up with this list to find the top states:

- *Total sales per state*

- *Total sales per million residents (per state)*, instead of *total sales per customer per state* (the metric the chosen by the marketing managers), since they were interested in assessing potential states for expansion of the customer base, not existing customers

- *90th percentile of sales by state*—these are the top five states to target

Note that the second and third metrics contrast the differences per state.

Helpful Hint
The order in which you create your presentation may differ from that shown here. For instance, you may already have the most useful metrics in your analysis. Also, order topics logically in the final presentation. For instance, start with simple metrics and progress to complex ones.

ATTRACTIVE VISUALS

Being attractive and being credible can and do go together.

—LISA GUERRERO
Sportscaster and former cheerleader, Los Angeles Rams

If you want your audience to understand your results, don't forget to ask yourself: "Is this the right chart?" The right chart is not only the appropriate chart type; it also displays the correct metrics and data. As an overall guideline, remember to use tables for details/precision and graphs for overall shape or trends in the data. However, selecting the right chart is extensively covered in the analysis portions of this book, *The Fifth and Sixth C's.*

Once you've determined that you have the right chart, get ready to show it to colleagues by ensuring that the chart is attractive but useful. An "attractive" chart means more than being pleasant to look at; it also means that your message is being clearly delivered to your audience.

This list can help you better understand what attractive means.

Helpful Hint

Companies often have standardized Power Point templates or perhaps even graph templates that you must use for slide shows.

Do the best you can to make the important information stand out, and if the chart is inappropriate for your data and questions, show an alternate version alongside it.

choose questions

collect data

check

clean

chart analysis

custom

communicate results

To give your story top billing:

Avoid "chart junk"

Flashy details, busy backgrounds, 3-D, animation, shadows, and weird chart angles distract the audience from your main story. Even if your data analysis software offers these features, resist the temptation to use them. Simple charts that clearly "shout out" your important results are the best.

Highlight and emphasize what's important

Avoid unnecessary details so that your audience can quickly understand the point of the chart.

Select useful colors and symbols

- Easy-to-understand meanings: using green for positive results, such as revenue, and red for negative results, such as spending, or upward arrows for increases and downward arrows for decreases, makes your charts easier to understand.
- Consistency: if possible, use the same color or symbol in a particular way throughout the presentation. For instance, if blue represents male customers, don't also use blue for married customers, or green for men in a different graph.
- Follow company standards: if a symbol or color is typically used in particular situations, use it the same way to reduce confusion.

Create meaningful titles for chart and axes.

Use titles that the audience would understand without your presence to explain them.

Label the units on your axes.

Numbers without the proper units can be misinterpreted, such as U.S. Dollars instead of Euros, or units sold versus thousands of units sold.

Case Study: Attractive visuals

Maria chose the appropriate charts for her metrics, and designed them effectively using the guidelines in the previous chapters. She also kept them clear and easy-to-read.

> **Helpful Hint**
>
> This topic in particular, designing attractive but useful graphs and tables, is covered in detail in some excellent books—see the *Further Reading* section for titles.

choose questions

collect data | check | clean

chart | analysis | custom

communicate results

ACTIONABLE INSIGHTS, RECOMMENDATIONS, AND DECISIONS

*In any moment of decision,
the best thing you can do is the right thing,
the next best thing is the wrong thing,
and the worst thing you can do is nothing.*

—THEODORE ROOSEVELT
First American to win a Nobel Prize and
26th President of the U.S.

Making recommendations based on your understanding of the business situation is one of an analyst's key roles. There are likely many factors beyond your understanding or scope of knowledge, so don't take it personally if the decision-maker questions you about your recommendations or decides upon a different route.

You will have met your goal if you informed your audience and influenced decision-making with the facts. At the end of the process, you are most likely not the "owner" of the area of interest, just a "navigator" pointing out the best course based on the available data.

Don't forget to mention the **limitations** of your analysis, which may include:

- *limited data* availability
- *poor data* quality
- *further data available* but not yet examined
- *quick-and-dirty analysis* done in a short time period
- the need for *more time* to perform a thorough review
- *highly volatile outcomes* over time

If you aren't immersed in the details of this area of the business, it's common to discover key information that would have been useful, but wasn't shared with you until after you presented your findings. It's also typical to have requests for further analysis based on new information that surfaces after your presentation. This is usually a good thing—your analysis has engaged your colleagues so that they are interested in finding out more.

Heads Up

Be careful that what you write does not offend anybody
or cause problems within the company.
The safest approach is to remove all useful information.

—SCOTT ADAMS
creator of the Dilbert comic strip

This is an exaggeration, but in delicate situations where people have a stake in a particular outcome, tact is always useful. Pointing out the positives of someone's work, especially before the negatives, is a good strategy. For instance, even though someone's pet project was an abject failure, try to share some positive finding before the long list of negatives.

Case Study: Actionable insights, recommendations and decisions

Based on the metrics used, Maria chose the top eight states with respect to potential sales growth. These included the five states in the top 90th percentile of sales, plus three alternate states to provide more options, if necessary. She also provided estimates of growth potential for these eight states, along with how she selected them.

To help the marketing team prioritize among the top eight states, she gave them an estimate of highest growth potential. Far and away, the best state is California, and the next tier of states includes Texas, New York, and Florida.

Heads Up

People are often in a rush to meet a deadline, or have spent so much time and energy on the rest of the analysis, that communicating the results is often an afterthought.

Try not to make this all-too-common mistake. A great analysis is not worth much if no one else understands what you've done! If you're able to plan ahead, leave enough time to review what you've done, especially if you are able to put it down for a little while and come back with a fresh approach.

choose questions
collect data
check
clean
chart
analysis
custom
communicate results

ATTENTION-GRABBING STORYLINES

Tell the audience what you're going to say,
say it;
then tell them what you've said.

—DALE CARNEGIE
Best-selling author of
How to Win Friends and Influence People (1936)

Now it's time to get your story straight by compiling all the information into a cohesive and compelling presentation. Simplicity is the key in any type of spoken or written business presentation! People are busy and you have a limited amount of time to get your point across. Don't give too much information, just the very minimum to make your case (usually people will remember only 2-4 points).

Tell your story in a few clear steps:

- What were your questions?

- What did you do to answer them?

- What did you find, including limitations of findings?

- What do you recommend?

- What further work is required?

Feel free to include interesting or funny anecdotes or graphics—simple doesn't have to mean boring.

Slide Surplus

This topic requires its own section, because one of the worst offenses by speakers is to jam in way too many slides for the time available—and most of us have done this at some point. People overdo it on the slides for a variety of reasons. They are excited about sharing all of the work that they've done, are nervous speakers so they feel more relaxed with all of the details in front of them, lack confidence in their decisions, or ran out of time during preparation and couldn't sort through the information, so they kept it all.

For instance, if you are preparing for a ten-minute speaking slot, only about five slides—yes, **five** slides—are necessary. A 45-minute talk requires only about twenty slides. Also, remember that complex charts take more time for people to process, and always leave time at the end for questions. If you must, stick all the interesting details, methodology, and other minutiae in the back of the slide deck in case someone is interested in discussing them after the talk.

If you happen to finish a few minutes early, that's not a bad thing. An audience rarely complains about a talk being too short!

Heads Up

You may have to pass around a copy of the slide show as a reference, or for people who weren't at the talk.

If you are concerned that readers won't understand what happened if the slides are too simple, supplement them with comments, perhaps by using the notes function in PowerPoint. Some people don't like reading notes, so another option is to create two versions when you are compiling the slide deck. Add slides with simple text (perhaps bulleted) of the details necessary for comprehension and save it. Then remove the excess slides and save a second version for the talk (where you can include notes for yourself, if you like).

choose questions

collect data

check

clean

chart

custom

analysis

communicate results

Helpful Hint

*No one who achieves success does so
without acknowledging the help of others.
The wise and confident acknowledge this help with gratitude.*

—ALFRED NORTH WHITEHEAD
British mathematician and "analytic" philosopher

If colleagues contributed work or ideas towards your analysis, remember to give them credit.

Case Study Finale: Maria pulls it all together

Maria uses the information that she compiled to tell the story about her analysis using a short slide presentation.

Download her slides in color at www.AccidentalAnalyst.com .

RECAP OF THE SEVENTH C:
COMMUNICATE YOUR RESULTS

- Pull all the other C's together to effectively communicate your results.

- Presentation types include slide shows, discussions during group meetings, e-mails, memos, or written reports.

- The goal of your analysis is to help people take action in their areas of the business.

- Straight "A" benchmarks to evaluate your presentations:

    — Audience-appropriate results

    — Answers to the right questions

    — Applicable metrics

    — Attractive visuals

    — Actionable insights, recommendations, and decisions

    — Attention-grabbing storylines

Remember to download a sample, full-color slide presentation at www.AccidentalAnalyst.com

FURTHER READING

Data, Analysis and Statistics

Schaums Outline of Statistics, Murray J. Spiegel, Larry J. Stephens, 2011.

How to Lie with Statistics, Darrell Huff, 1993.

Stat-Spotting: A Field Guide to Identifying Dubious Data, Joel Best, 2008.

Charts and Data Visualization

Show Me the Numbers: Designing Tables and Graphs to Enlighten, Stephen Few, 2012.

The Visual Display of Quantitative Information, Edward Tufte, 1995.

Rapid Graphs with Tableau Software 7, Stephen McDaniel and Eileen McDaniel, 2012.

Rapid Dashboards Reference Card, Stephen McDaniel and Eileen McDaniel, 2010. Details at www.freakalytics.com/rdrc, available as a laminated card on Amazon and as an app on the Android, iPad, and iPhone.

Communication

Presentation Zen, Garr Reynolds, 2008.

Enchantment: The Art of Changing Hearts, Minds, and Actions, Guy Kawasaki, 2008.

INDEX

ACKNOWLEDGEMENTS

Content Reviewer: *Jeff Mills*

Copyeditor: *Heidi Fuchs*

Cover Art: *Stephen McDaniel*

We'd like to thank the many people that have been excited about this book since we started writing it—here's a list of a few of them. Professor Pat Hanrahan at Stanford University discussed ideas and gave us great advice. I-Kong Fu, Suzi King, and Steven Kurian (from Down Under!) contributed useful feedback. Lynzi Ziegenhagen and Dan Benevento from Aspire Public Schools gave us great tips on file sharing and documentation. Annabelle Laramee kindly evaluated our cover design.

For teaching her how to analyze real-world data, Eileen would like to thank the "stats guru" Jack Weiss for his patience, along with Flora Lu and Seth Reice (who are both warm and wonderful people!). Eileen was inspired by Jim Prost and Douglas "Mac" MacLachlan for their enthusiasm about marketing. Special thanks to Jacqui and Ian Taylor (our British counterparts!), Monica and Raymond Gordon, Lisa Davenport and John Terborgh, Craig Duncan and Shayne Covert.

Finally, we would like to thank the many people who have read our books and attended our talks and training seminars over the years. You have been extremely kind with your feedback, enthusiasm and support.

Made in the USA
San Bernardino, CA
09 February 2020